HEROES AND VILLAINS
KEVIN GREENE

www.facebook.com/heroesandvillainsbook
kgreene.deviantart.com

It seems like I've always been a fan of sci-fi.

When I was a kid I used to visit my dad's job in Manhattan and work with him on some weekends and during the summer. My father was the superintendent of an office building on 7th Avenue- 3 Penn Plaza, diagonally across from Madison Square Garden and Penn Station - and whenever there was a new tenant moving their business in, my brother and I would go and help knock down walls and paint and stuff like that. Mostly we would hang out and watch our father interact with the oddballs that worked in the building or visited. Eventually my brother got older (he's four years ahead of me), so he would do his own thing and I would go by myself and work/ hang out. And when the day was over, after my dad had gotten me my Blimpie burger and Pepsi for lunch, he would take me over to Barnes and Noble, which used to be on 7th between 34th and 33rd. I still remember how that place looked. I still remembered how it SMELLED, like... well, books, I guess. It had two entrances, one on 7th and one on 33rd, with a little ramp leading to the 33rd side. And my dad would set me loose to get whatever book I wanted. A lot of times it was comic strip books, like Peanuts or Quincy or something like that... but just as many times it was pulp novels, like Conan or Tarzan or The Avenger or Star Trek episode novelizations by James Blish OR, most notably, Doc Savage. I must have (still) about thirty Doc Savage books, mostly with the COOL James Bama covers (what an artist). Doc Savage was crazy thirties sci-fi, with nutty villains and insane machines... I loved it. And my dad would just buy it, no problem, and we would go home. The only time he said anything was when I was reading and walking into the street. I guess it was read what you want but don't get killed doing it, stupid.

Science fiction was big for me on the screen as well. My brother and I discovered *Star Trek* on Channel 11 at six o'clock and was like, "What the hell is THIS?" It made a bigger impression on me than my brother, though. During the summer my mother was fine with me staying up to watch TV until all hours. *Trek, The Twilight Zone, Voyage to the Bottom of The Sea*... and then the movies. Monster Week and Science Fiction week on the 4:30 Movie on Channel Seven (as long as I got my homework done!), Chiller Theater on Saturday nights and all those crazy 50's sci-fi and horror movies. While everyone else in my house was asleep I was up to all hours watching all kinds of nonsense. And going to the the movies... my mother took me to see *Star Wars, Superman, Close Encounters of the Third Kind*... and she had zero (if possible, less than zero) interest in any of that stuff. But she let me watch what I wanted to watch and draw my little pictures.

Then, in 1975 (I think), all of these things collided in one event, courtesy of my older sister Paula. She took me to a Creation Convention at the Pennsylvania Hotel (across from Penn Station... I've spent my whole life around that area) and the top of my head blew off. I got a GREAT poster by John Buscema of all the best Marvel characters (wish I still had that.. it took a beating over the years) and all kinds of books and comics and art. We watched four straight *Doctor Who* episodes with Tom Baker. We wandered the floor and met artists and looked at starship models and thumbed through comic long boxes. All kinds of stuff. I don't think my sister was super interested but she let me just lose my mind in there. She seemed to enjoy herself watching me enjoy myself. Paula always encouraged me to embrace the unusual, the "off the beaten path". She was about as good an older sister a young comic book, sci-fi geek could hope for. I realize now the impact they had on me, their encouraging me to be who I am. My parents letting a 14 year old budding artist ride a subway by himself everyday from Brooklyn to Manhattan to go to an art high school. Because he really wanted to go. And even though I clearly wasn't going to be the architect my mother hoped for, they let me go and draw my pictures and meet other good friends who grew up like me; it's good knowing there are others, a community. And my sister there as well, encouraging and guiding me the whole time.

Well, here we are years later and my mother, father and sister are all gone, those moments with them still there but the details fading. I have a wife and a son now, and he's an unusual little dude. I see what my family had to deal with. I try not to push my likes and hobbies on him (except for the Mets. They need all the support they can get) but he seems to naturally skew towards the fantastic. And recently, when I was collecting *Star Trek* reference, he walked up to my computer and said, out of the clear blue, "It's Captain Kirk. And Mr Spock. And the *Enterprise*!" And he smiled at me.

I tell you, I had to fight back some serious geek tears there.

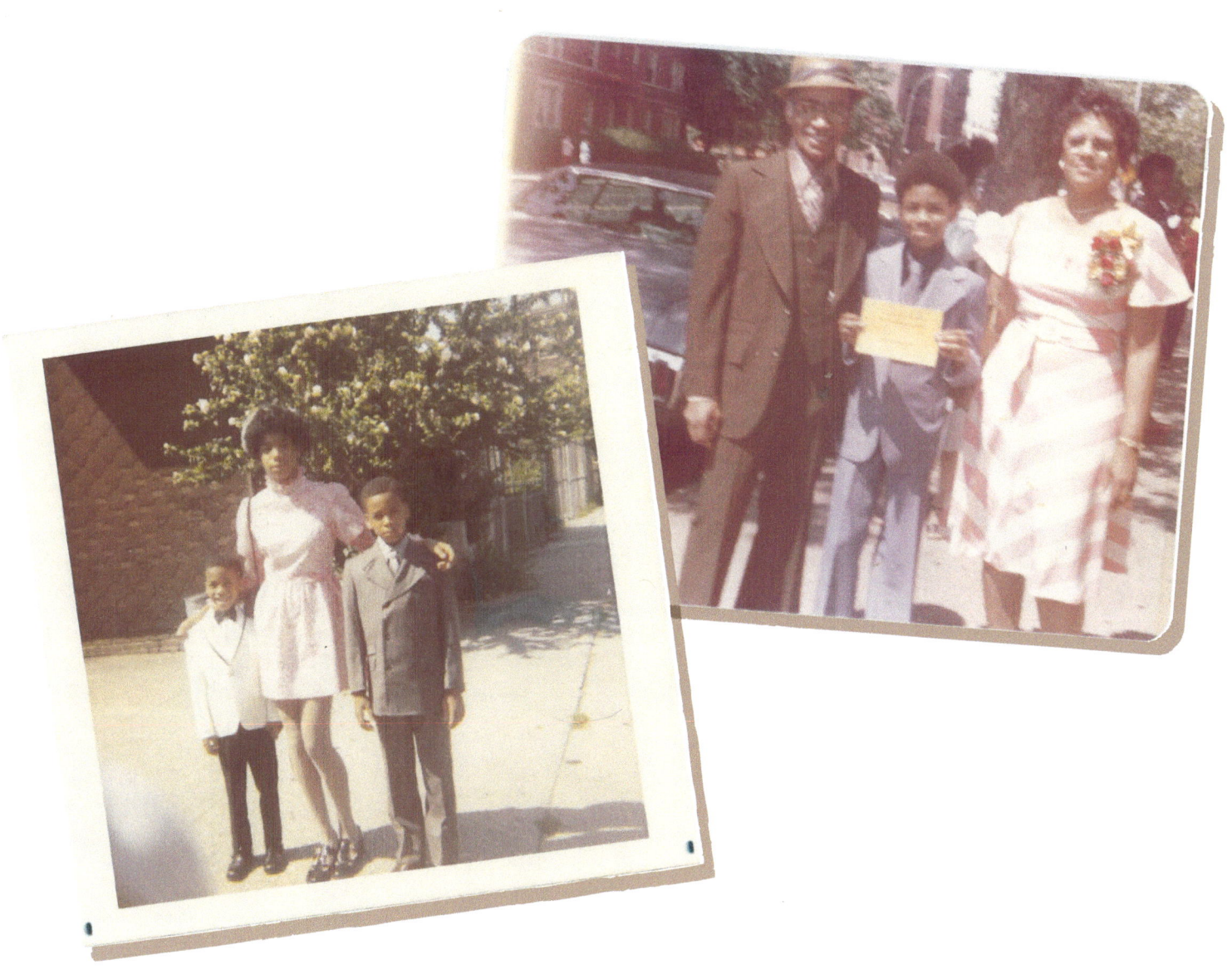

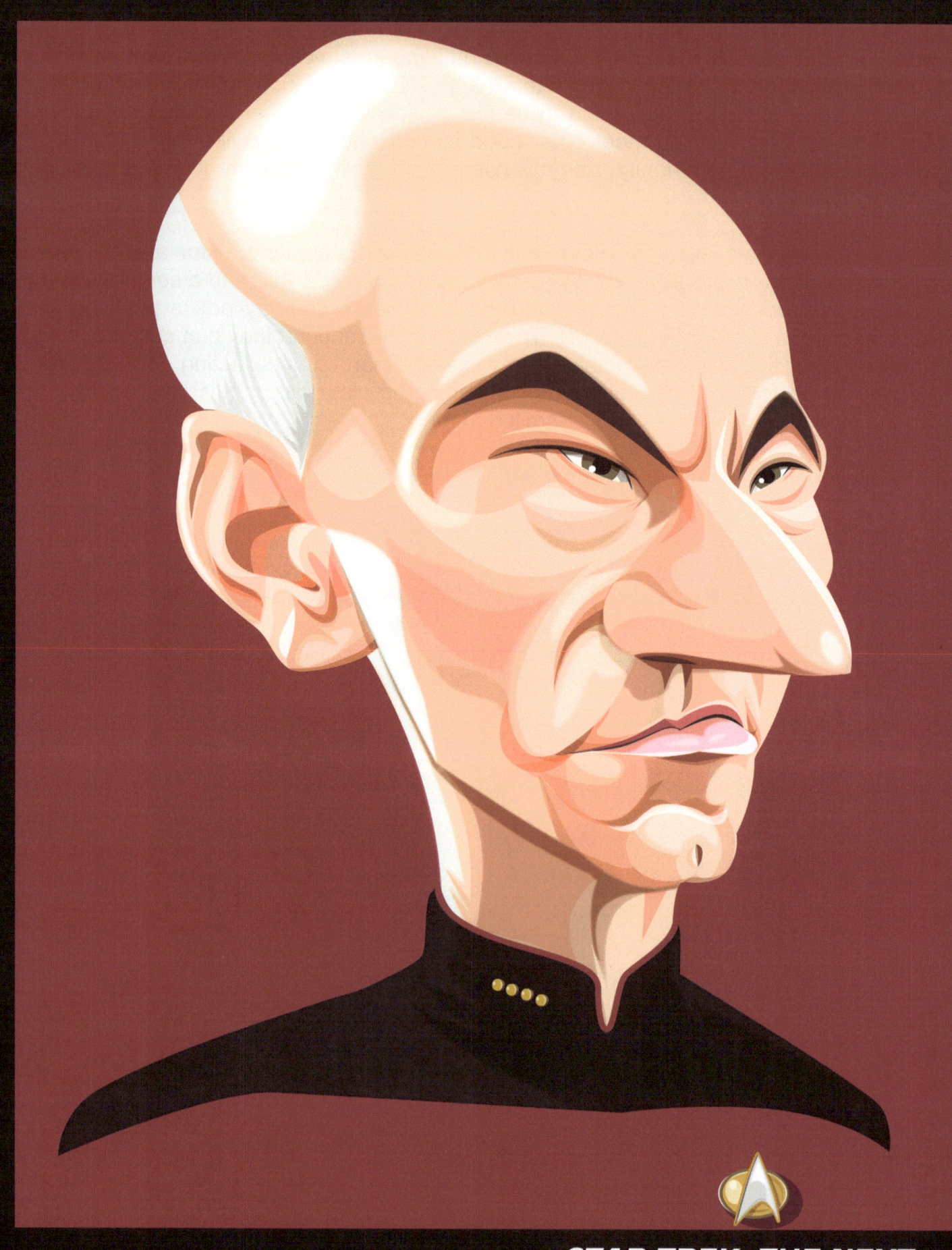

CAPTAIN JEAN-LUC PICARD —— *STAR TREK: THE NEXT GENERATION (1987-1994)*

Easily one of my all-time favorite television characters. Picard, as portrayed by Patrick Stewart, may not have had the physicality or the charming ego of Captain Kirk but his quiet leadership and vocal command made him, in my opinion, just as cool. I'd say this is Picard from about the third season of The Next Generation, when the show started to come together for good. From that point on we had great Picard-centric episodes like "Family", "Darmok", "The Inner Light", "Chain of Command Part II" and others where Stewart shined (that wasn't a "four lights" pun). He may not have ever drop-kicked anyone but he's still a great captain.

GENERAL ZOD — SUPERMAN II (1980)

They might've played General Zod a little bit for laughs but Terrance Stamp as Zod really gave you the impression that he took himself very seriously. He was funny without really trying to be, all arrogant and regal but he meant business. "Kneel before Zod!" is still a great line (I wonder how many people say it to Stamp weekly) and he's a great villain, though I wish he was a little more bad, a little more evil. No matter; General Zod is still a good baddie, 70's shiny suit and all.

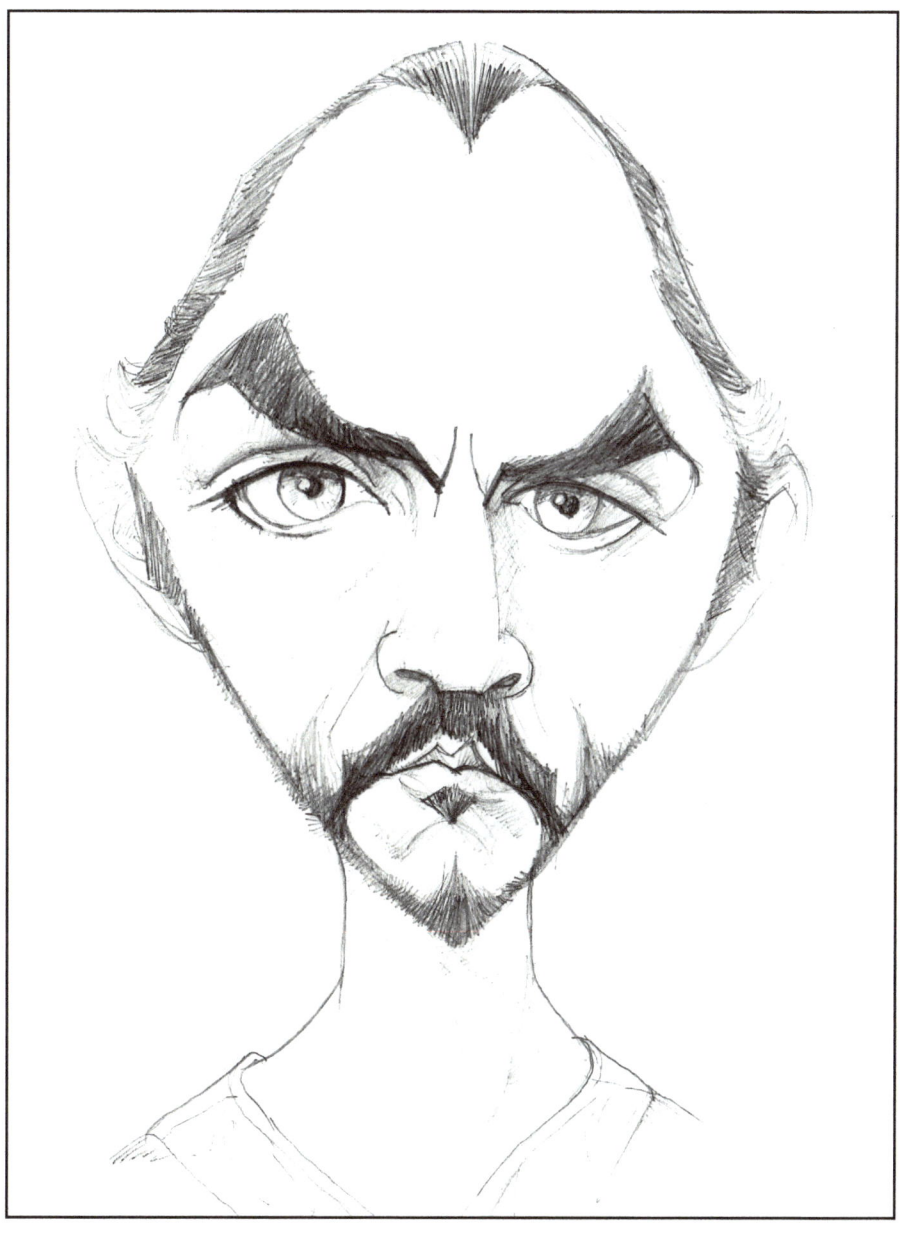

One of the great characters of science fiction, much less a great female character, Ellen Ripley went through some serious stuff dealing with aliens and just trying to get home. Sigourney Weaver (the Queen of Sci-Fi) said she would like to play Ripley again... I say let her. Everyone loves Sigourney. Let's ignore the last two movies and take it from *Aliens*. How? No idea. But I'd love to see them try...

I saw *Aliens* at the (defunct) Kingsway Theater on Kings Highway in Brooklyn. Double date. Me, my girlfriend ShawnTina and another couple. To this day I still laugh at this: Before all hell breaks loose there are a couple of very tense moments with the Colonial Marines searching for the colonists in the processing station. Creepy. Getting more tense by the second. And Shawntina leans over to me and whispers "I think I'm having a heart attack!" Over twenty five years ago and that little moment still amuses me.

SCORPIUS — FARSCAPE (1999-2003)

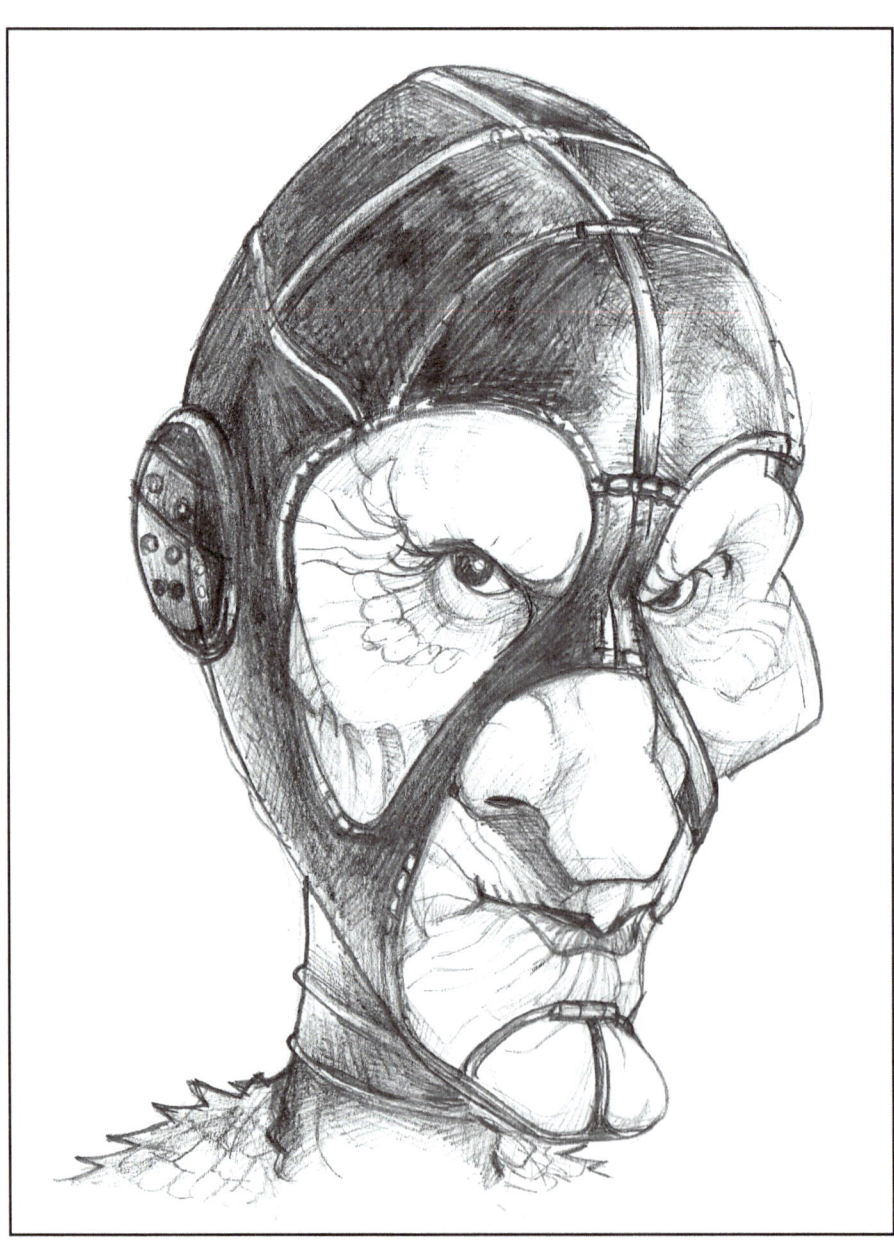

If I could vote for the most underrated television show in history (and any kind of show, too, not just science fiction), it would be for *Farscape*. I almost never hear this show mentioned when great television sci-fi is discussed and that's just plain wrong. *Farscape* is easily one of the best. Easily. It certainly looked like no show before it or since. And I always say it has the highest "Oh sh&!" factor of any program I've ever seen. That, and the highest "I can't BELIEVE they just did that" factor as well. A big part of both those factors is the great villain of the show, Scorpius, as played by Wayne Pygram. A hybrid of two warring species, Scorpius, who was introduced in the show's 19th episode, is as devious, calculating and dangerous a bad guy as you'll ever see on the small screen. I mean, just look at him. No seriously, go get the DVD's and look at him. You'll love to hate him.

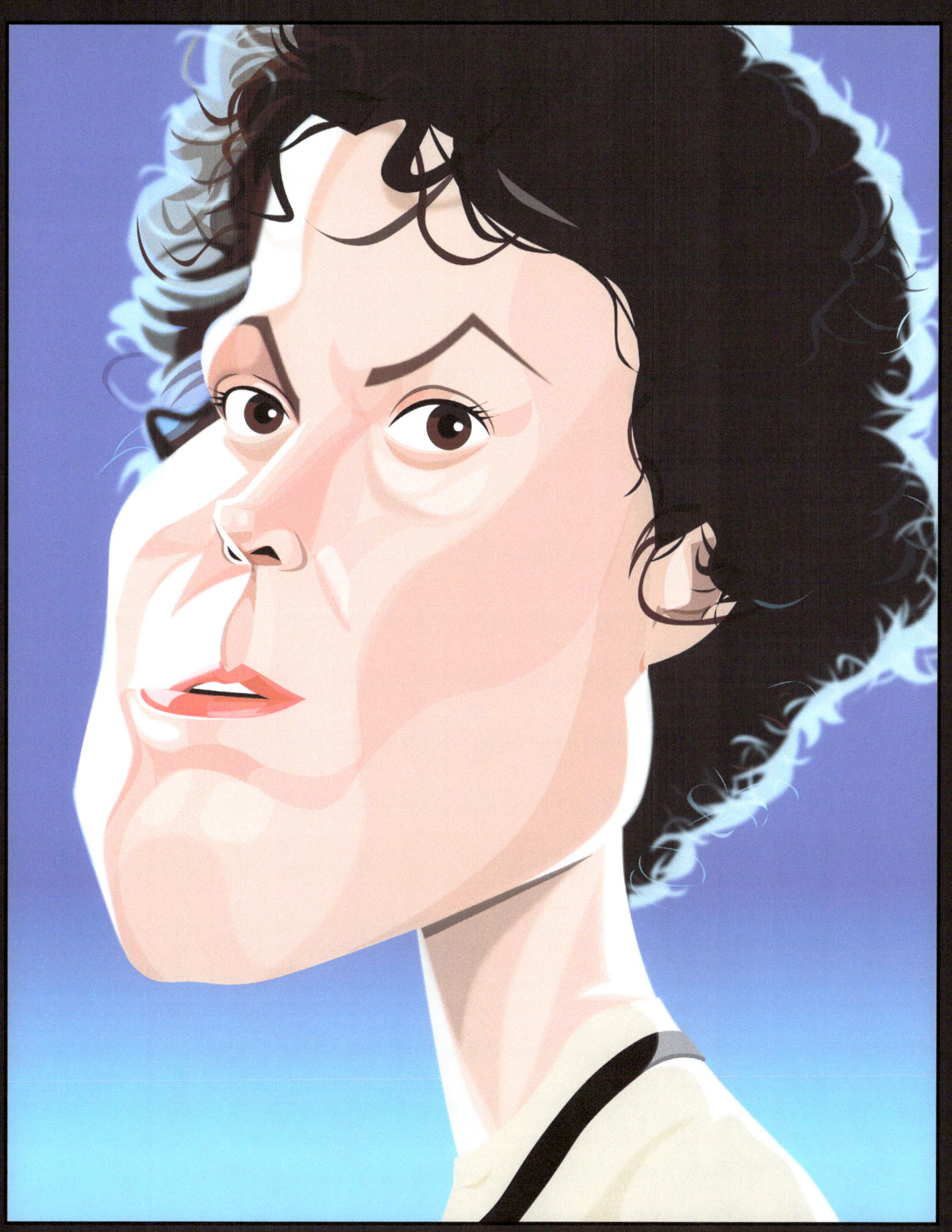

LT. ELLEN RIPLEY ——— *ALIENS* (1986) ———

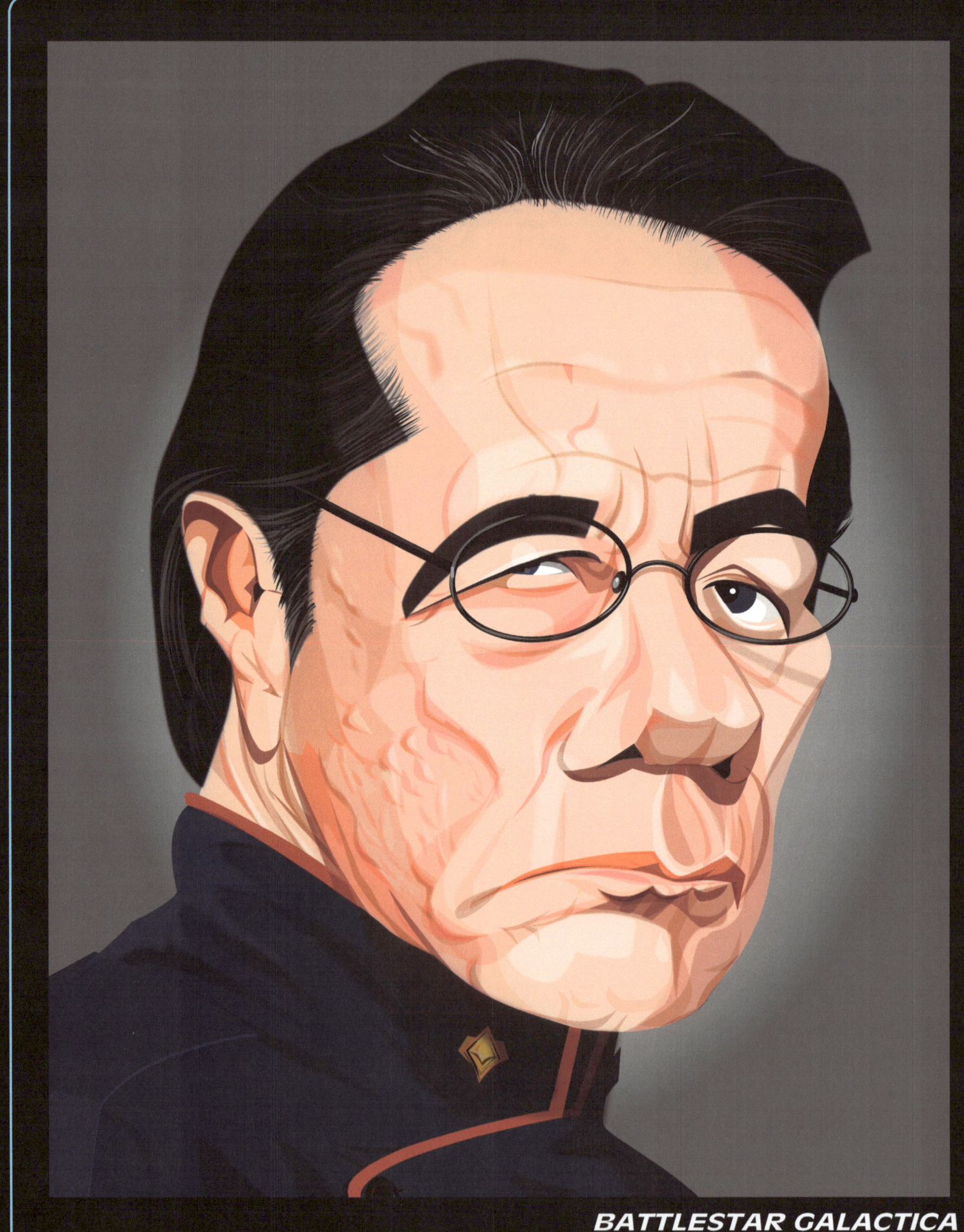

ADMIRAL WILLIAM ADAMA

BATTLESTAR GALACTICA
(2003-2008)

Admiral William Adama is another one of my favorite TV characters. He's more emotional than Captain Picard but they share the same quiet command persona that earns respect. There's a scene in the first episode "33" where Tigh loses it at Dualla and pretty much everyone because, during the continual attacks by the Cylons, one of the civilian fleet ships gets lost during a jump. After Tigh yells at everyone Adama really quietly says something to the effect of "We really can't afford any mistakes. There's not a lot of us left." And that had way more impact than Tigh going off.

Adama can be really stubborn but will admit when he was wrong, as he was with Apollo a bunch of times. But he always ended up doing the right thing in some really difficult situations. Just a very cool character.

KHAN NOONIEN SINGH — STAR TREK II: THE WRATH OF KHAN (1982)

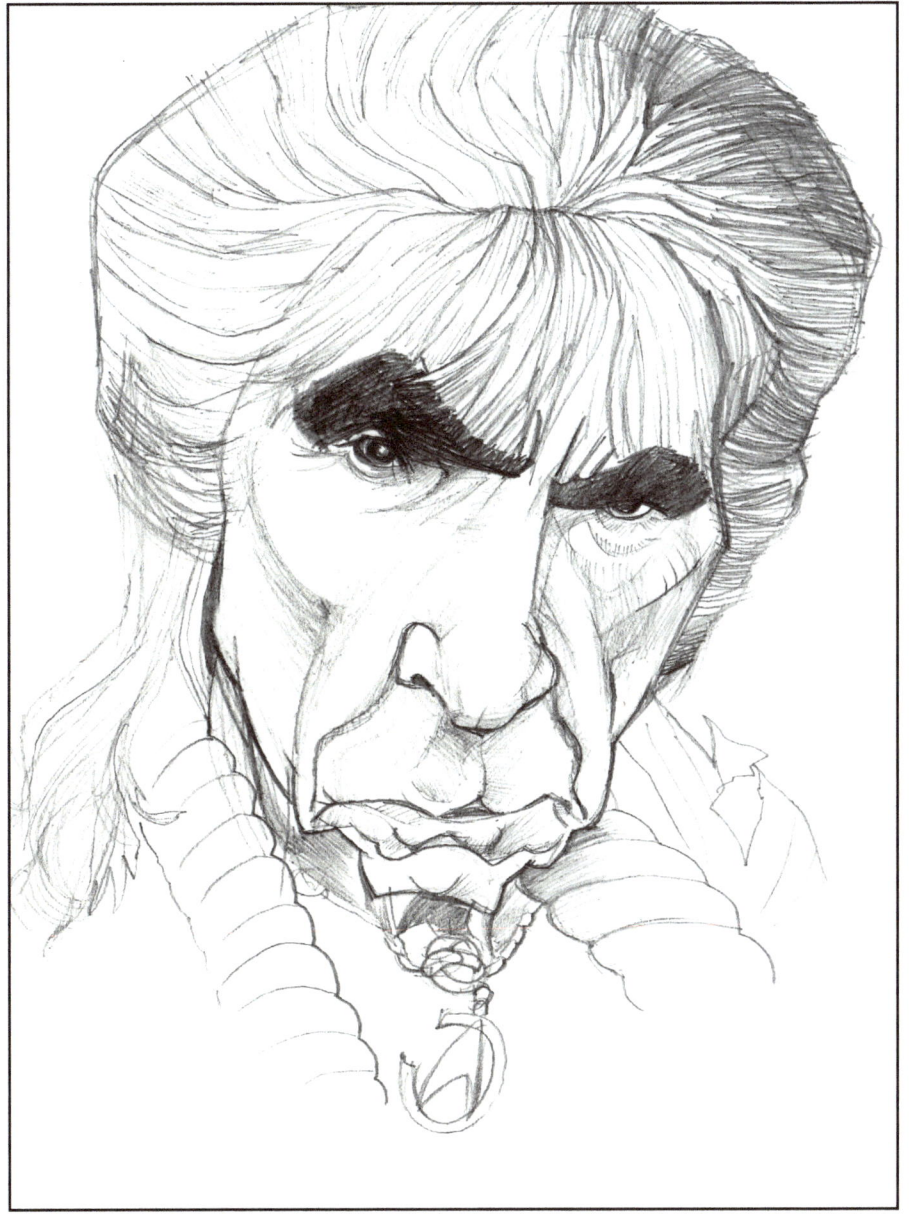

Here we are, 30 years after the premiere of *Star Trek II* and Khan is still the franchises' best villain. By the way, who's number two? The Borg Queen? Commander Kurn? Gary Mitchell? Who knows, maybe the villain (Khan?) from the next Trek film will finally take the top spot. But until then, this Khan is numero uno. Which is amazing considering that Khan and Kirk are never physically face to face in the film. But Khan is bad enough that he doesn't have to be. I love Ricardo Montalban in this movie. He's cocky and vengeful and arrogant and he gets to yell crazy sh*! like "Full power! DAMN YOU!" and make it sound good. There's one little shot that still makes me laugh. When the *Reliant* enters the Mutara Nebula and the ship is rocked, watch the dude standing behind Khan. He loses his balance, jostles Khan's shoulder and is all crazy apologetic when Khan shoots him the nastiest look.So funny. Even his crew wants no part of him...

OH yeah, I admit it. I was worried about this guy. I love David Tennant's Doctor and I was concerned about how this Matt Smith guy would fly. I needn't be concerned. About 5 minutes into his first episode I was starting to believe and by the time he walked through the projected image of David Tennant's face to claim the title of the 11th Doctor I was sold. Matt Smith has done a great job carrying the torch. I should've had more faith...

DR. ZACHARY SMITH — *LOST IN SPACE* (1965-1968)

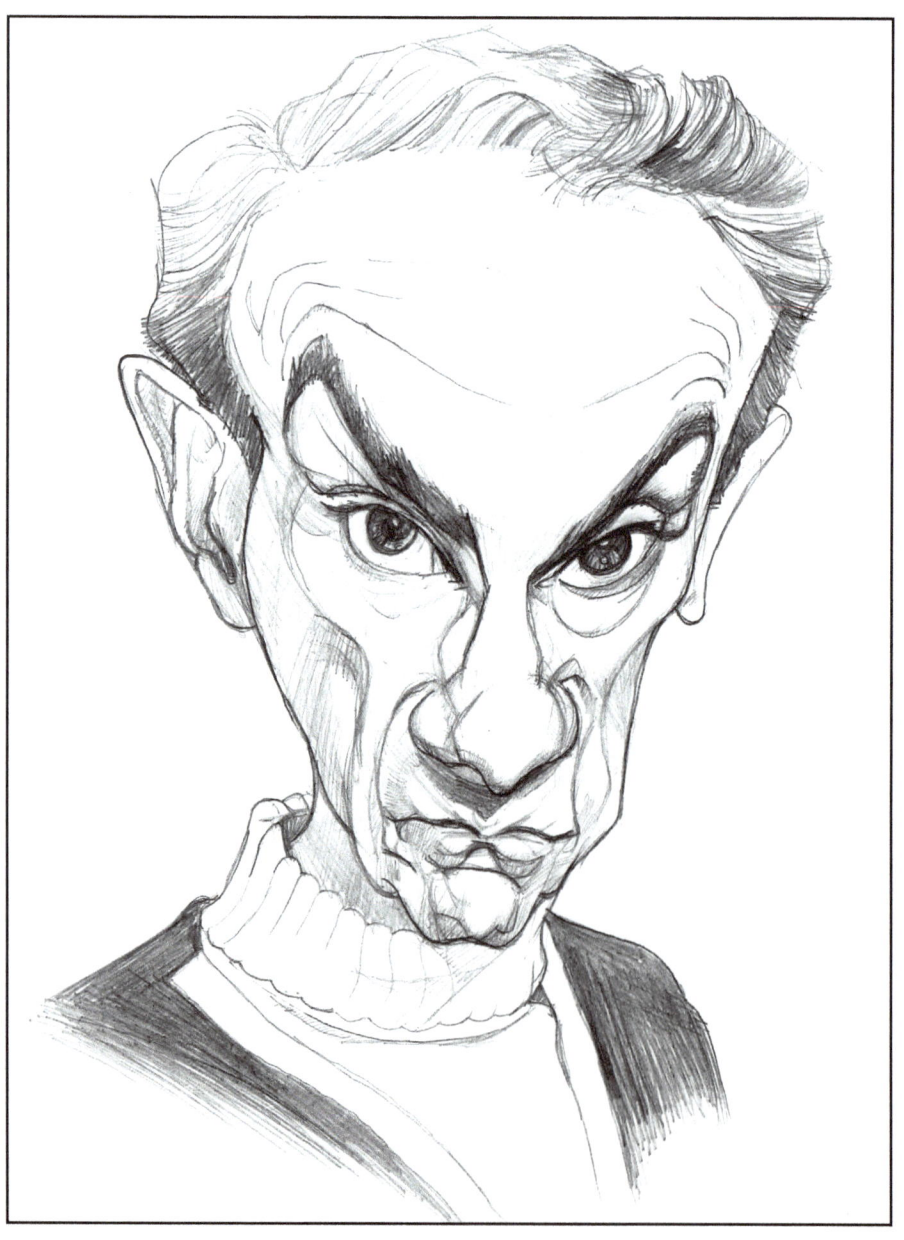

It's kind of odd to think it now but Dr. Smith was actually a pretty stone cold bad guy in the beginning of the show, especially the pilot. He was an enemy agent sent to sabotage the *Jupiter 2,* killing everyone aboard 8 hours after it's launch. But he accidentally got trapped on board and the ship survived, though they became hopelessly lost (hence the title). That kind of butts heads with the Dr. Smith that he would become; the cowardly, flamboyant, whining, self-serving jerk we all love. Jonathan Harris was encouraged to rewrite his lines and make Dr. Smith more interesting and somewhat sympathetic to the audience, He basically created Dr. Smith, the one everyone remembers, anyway. And that evil, potentially family-killing foreign agent villain was all but forgotten. Oh, the pain!

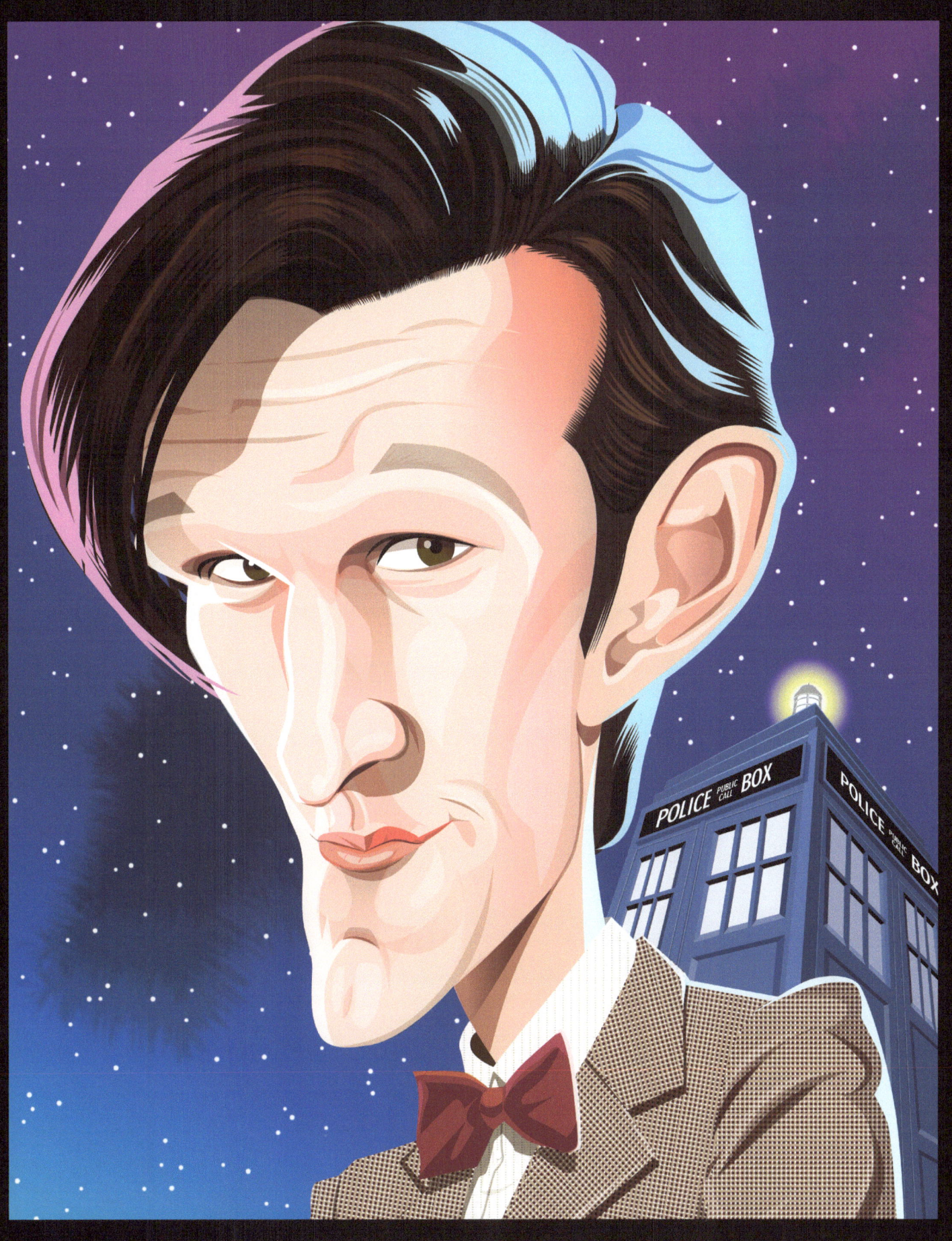

THE ELEVENTH DOCTOR — *DOCTOR WHO (2010-?)*

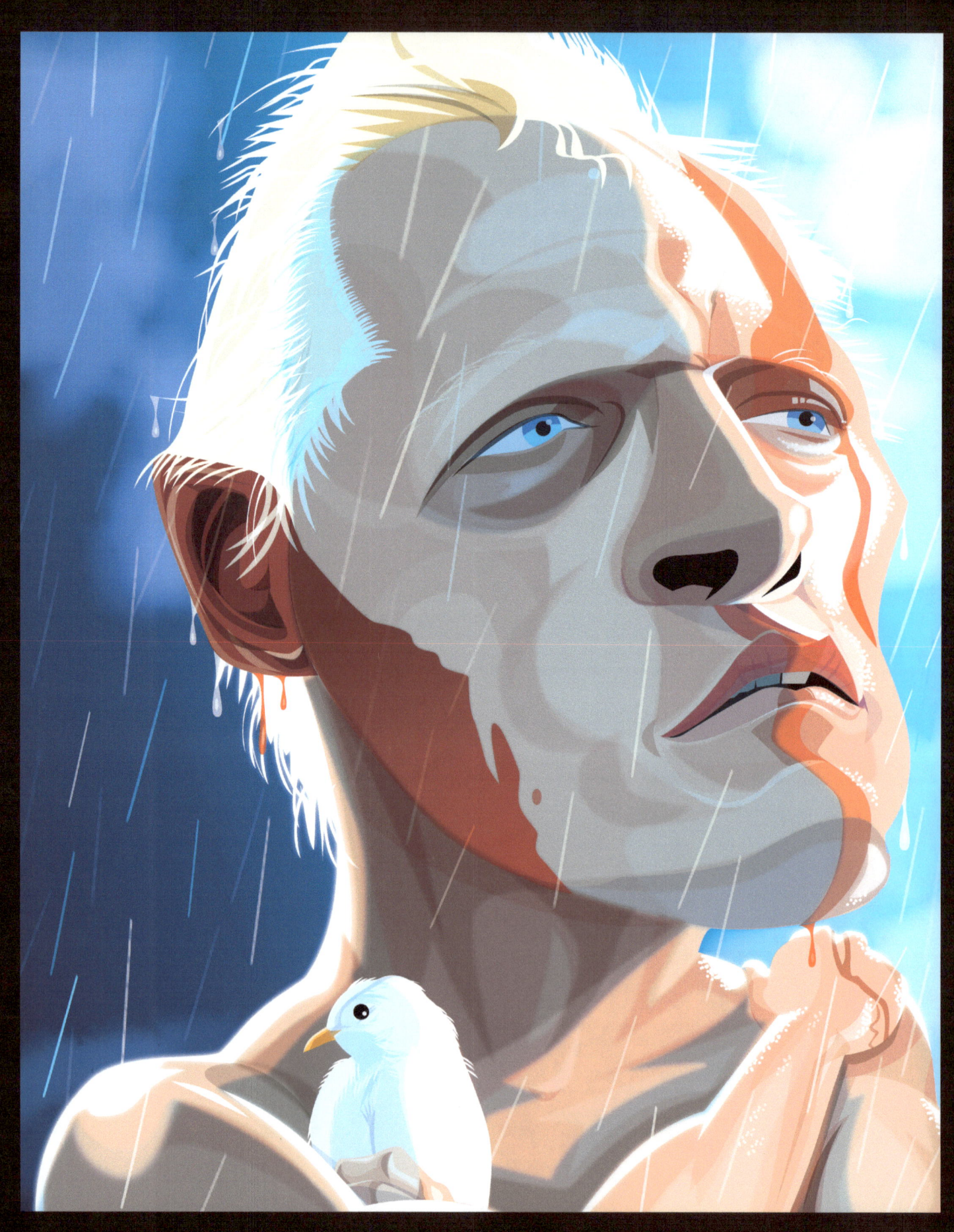

ROY BATTY —— *BLADERUNNER (1982)*

I always wished I could see the things that Roy Batty describes in his last moments of life. Attack ships on fire off the shoulder of Orion? That would be cool! Maybe the next film set in the *Blade Runner* universe should be about the adventures of an idealistic Roy Batty before finally realizing his mortality and turning murderous. The only problem with that would be that Rutger Hauer, who was fantastic as Batty and improvised much of the "Tears in Rain" speech, would be too old to play the part. Too bad. Hauer made Roy Batty one of the most sympathetic villains in movie history. After all, if you knew you were a machine with a set life span wouldn't you try to extend it?

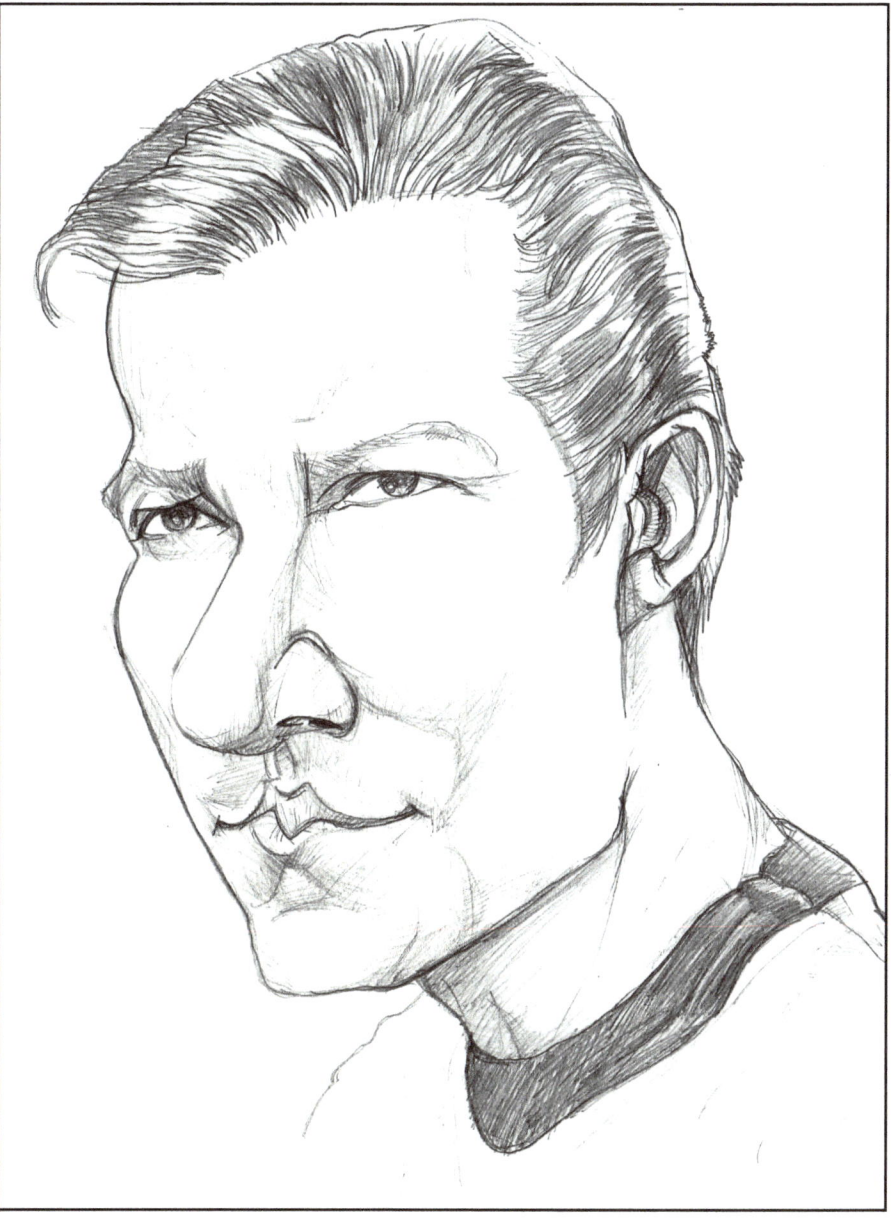

I said earlier that Captain Jean Luc Picard is one of my all time favorite television characters. And Captain Benjamin Sisko definitely made a great impression on me, being a strong black command figure in the *Star Trek* universe. But you have to give it up for Captain Kirk, for not only being the first *Trek* captain we saw but also being the ballsiest. Between drop kicking and karate chopping bad guys and bedding all the space chicks he could, Kirk talked not one, not two but THREE separate crazy computers into shutting themselves down. Later on in the movies he got promoted to Admiral, stole his own ship, blew it up, got busted back down to Captain and STILL got a new *Enterprise* out of the deal (I guess saving the planet... AGAIN...,does have it's perks). AND his middle name is Tiberius. Come on. That's pretty badass right there.

I always thought that Tarkin, as played by the great Peter Cushing, was one of the great *Star Wars* villains. I know, I know, he ain't Sith and he doesn't run around with a light saber or blasters... but my man blew up a whole planet just to make a point. THAT is hardcore.

My mother took me and my friend Katrell to see *Star Wars* at the Albermarle Theater on Flatbush Ave. I was twelve years old. My mother wasn't a fan of sci-fi but she actually made a joke during the movie. After Chewbacca let out some guttural howl my mother leaned over and said to us, in mock seriousness, "What did he say?" We cracked up. Twelve year olds find that kinda stuff hilarious.

MR SPOCK — STAR TREK (2009)

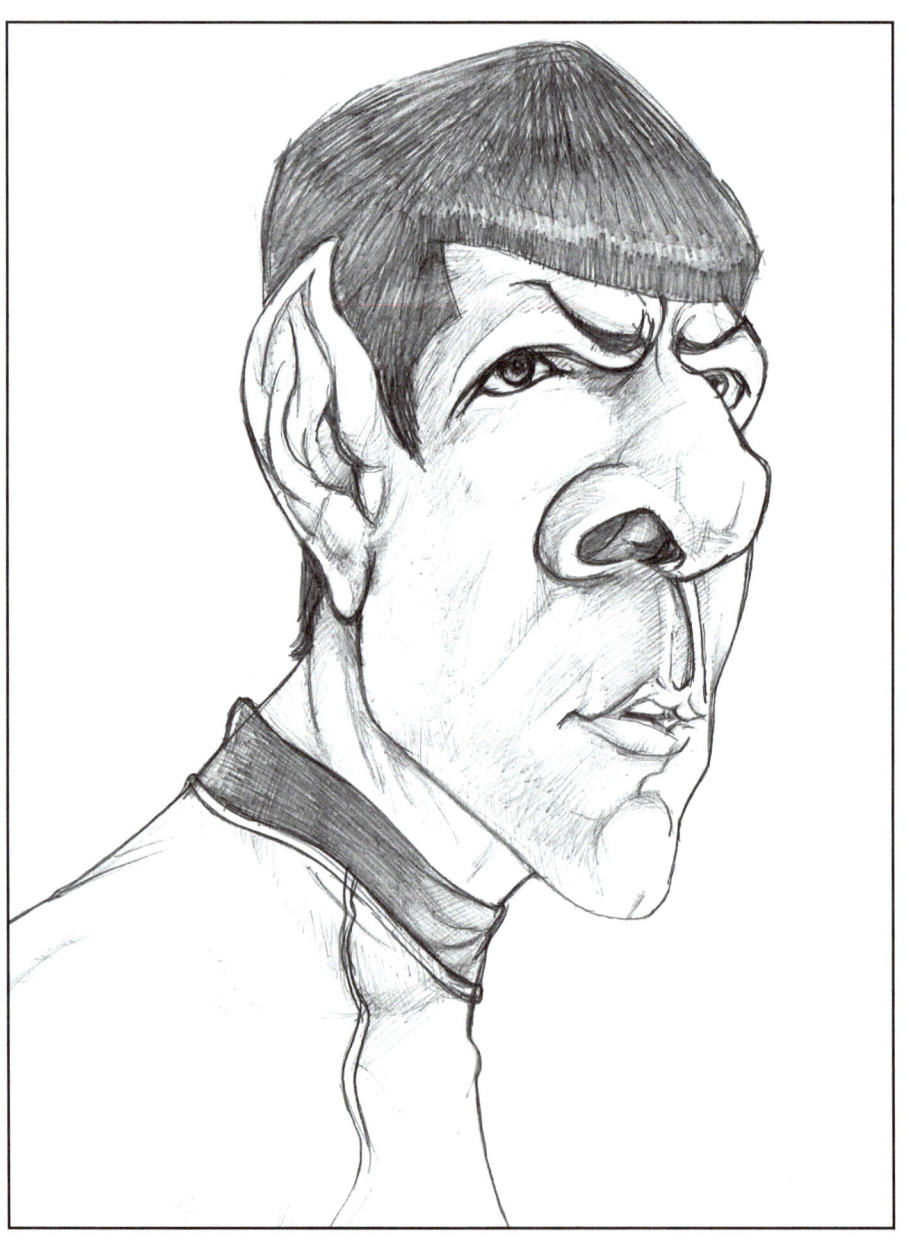

Leonard Nimoy's Spock was always cool and it was nice to see the coolness continue with Zachary Quinto's portrayal of everyone's favorite Vulcan. An aspect of Spock that I've always liked, especially when dealing with McCoy, is his sarcasm. Just subtle enough that it doesn't seem emotional but pointed enough to get the jab. Quinto did a nice job with that and also got to play Spock angry, which was always fun to see Nimoy do ("Right next to the dog-faced boy!"-that may be my friend Michael Boruch's favorite line from TOS. That and "It used to be! But not any more!!). AND he's dating Uhura. Yup. Spock is DEFINITELY cool.

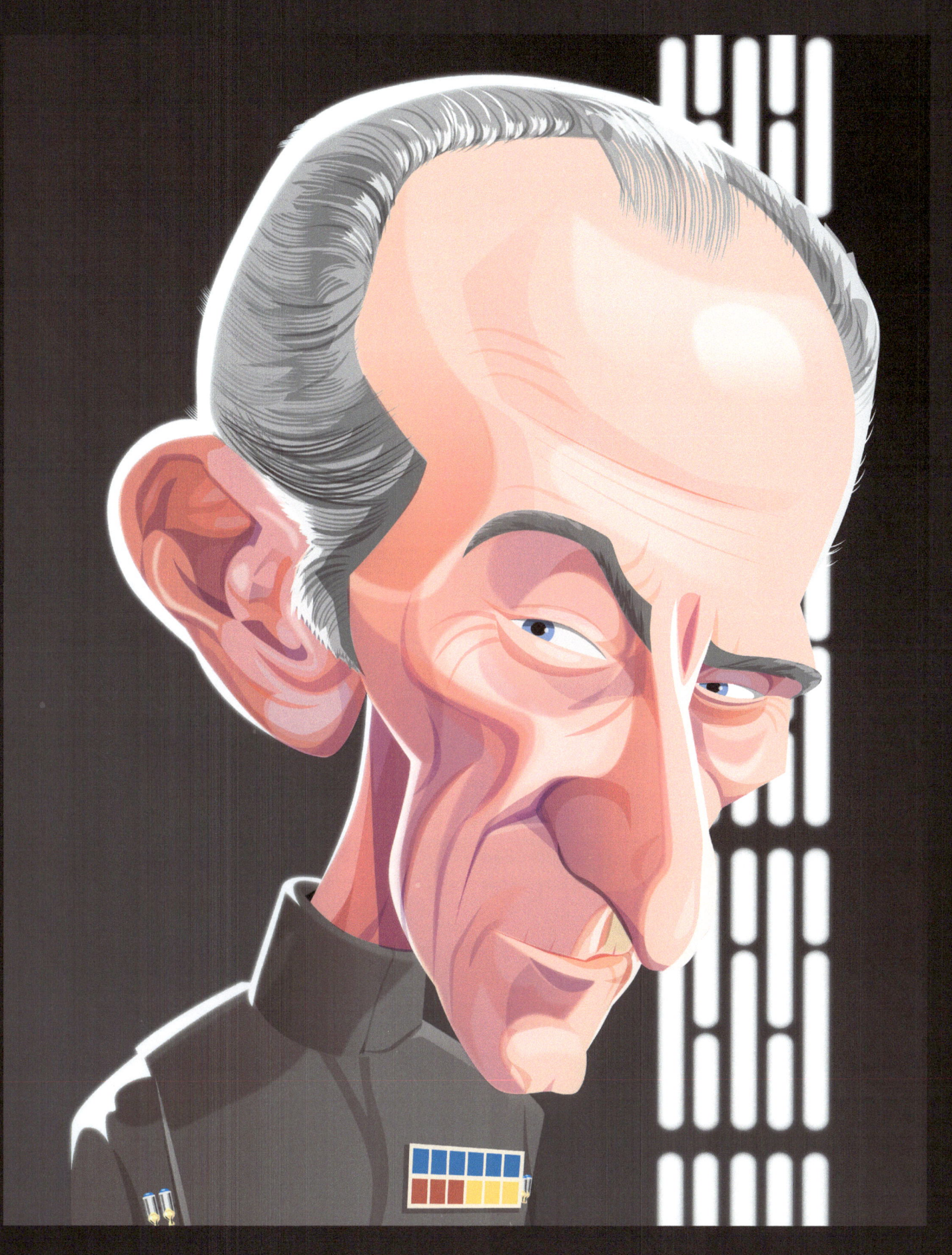

GRAN MOFF TARKIN —— STAR WARS (1977)

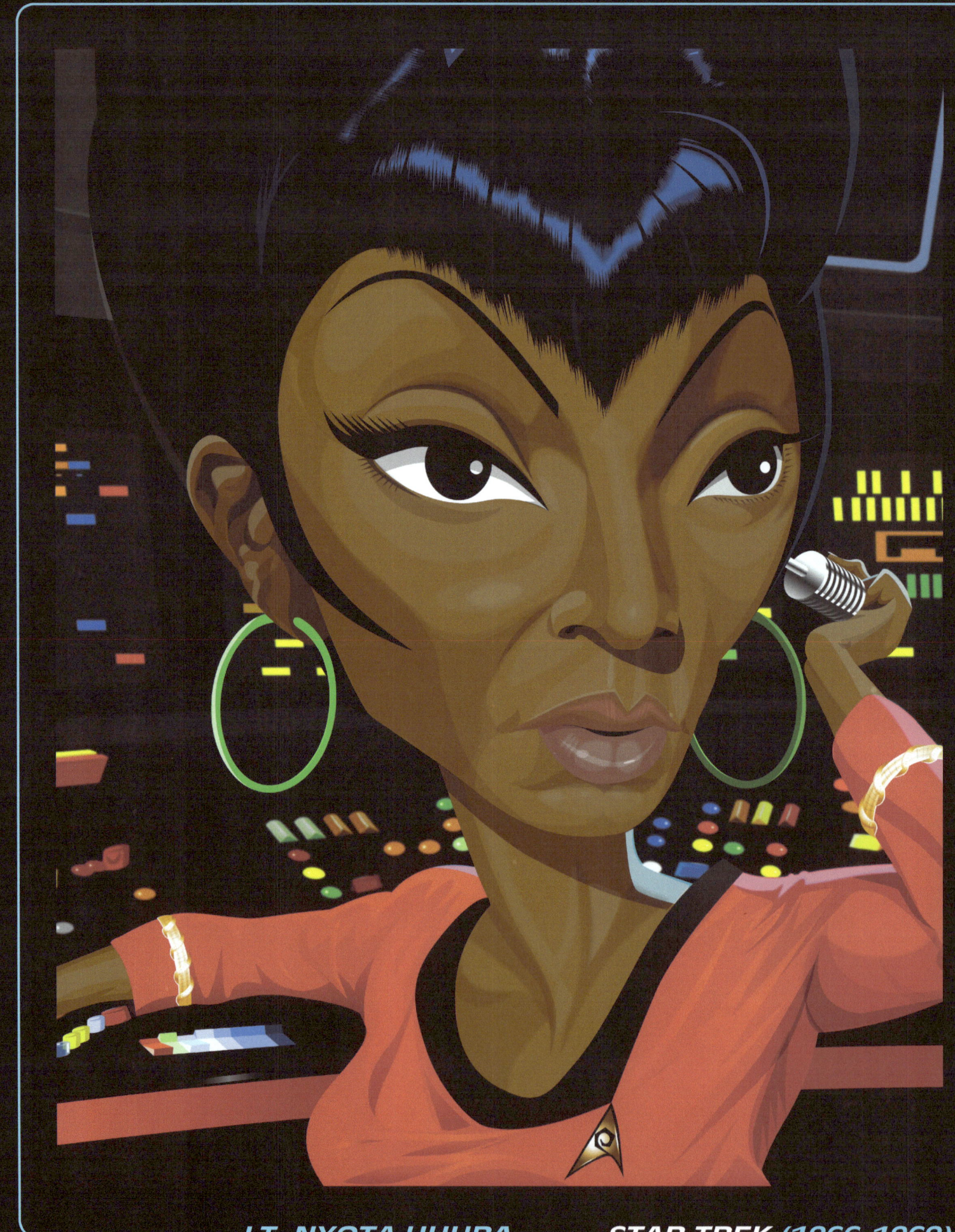

LT. NYOTA UHURA —— *STAR TREK* (1966-1969)

Whoopi Goldberg has always said that the character of Uhura, played by Nichelle Nichols, was an inspiration to her. It showed her that a black woman, in the future, could be an integral part of a starship crew. Well, I admit, Uhura didn't really inspire me in that fashion. I just thought she was HOT. Those eyes, that face, that bangin' body in a short Starfleet dress (and don't get me started on how she looks in the episode "Mirror Mirror"... YOW). She was undeniably smokin'. But she was a great Starfleet officer as well, dedicated, reliable, brave and smart. Great qualities. Being a complete knockout doesn't hurt either.

SEBASTIAN SHAW — **X-MEN:FIRST CLASS (2011)**

I'm sure a lot of people still think of Kevin Bacon as the *Footloose* guy, the goofy dancing guy. They obviously have not paid attention to the assortment of rapists, pedophiles, murderers and maniacs that this guy has played over the last twenty plus years. So taking on the role of not just any old supervillain but a Nazi, racist, sexist, mother murdering genocidal supervillain in the great *X-Man:First Class* was probably a walk in the park for Kevin Bacon. He probably read the script and was like "Is that all this guy does???".

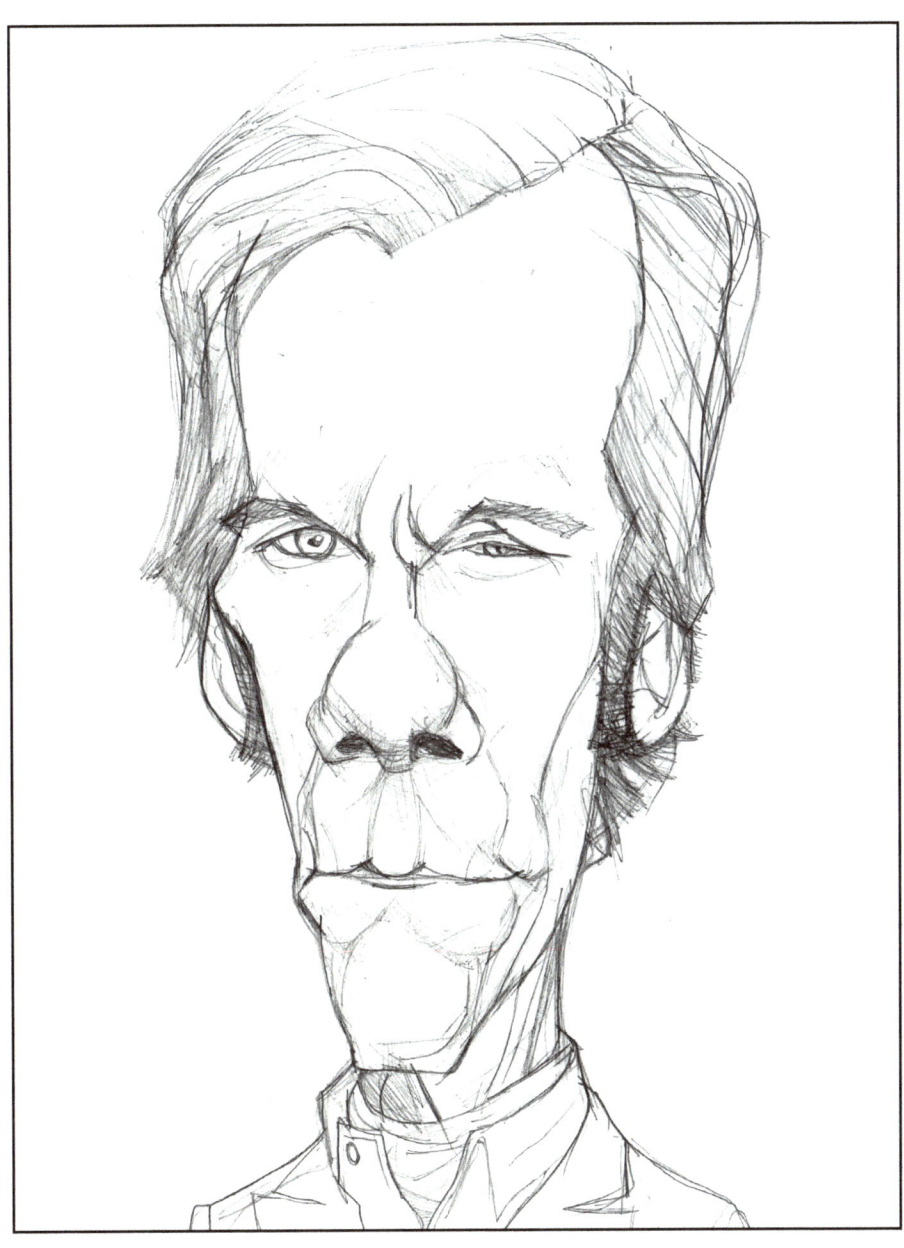

My mother took me to see *Superman* at the Kenmore Theater on Flatbush Ave. and Church (which is no longer there.. like pretty much all of the Brooklyn movie theaters from my youth). I was 13. This was probably the most anticipation I ever had for a movie. I knew a little about *Star Wars* before I saw it - I think the Marvel Comic adaption was out already - but an actual SUPERMAN movie? EVERYBODY knew Superman. And boy, this did not disappoint. And this relative unknown, this Christopher Reeve guy, who played Supes? GREAT. If he didn't sell it, the movie would've been a disaster. But he was amazing as Superman AND Clark Kent, becoming the benchmark forever.

Quick story. About a million years ago, it seems like, I was working at Paragon Sports, a big sporting goods store on 17th and 5th in Manhattan. And this one day, the crew I worked on was unloading these HEAVY treadmills from a truck, pushing them down a narrow hall and then to the warehouse. Grueling. So we're slaving away and who do we see walking towards us? Christopher Reeve and, I think, his family. So one of the guys says, "Hey Superman, how about you giving us a hand?" And Reeve smiled and said, "Sorry, fellas, it's my day off." We laughed and got back to work. It was a really small thing but it helped the day go by that much faster.

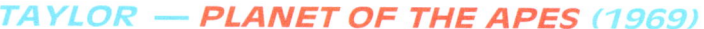

TAYLOR — PLANET OF THE APES (1969)

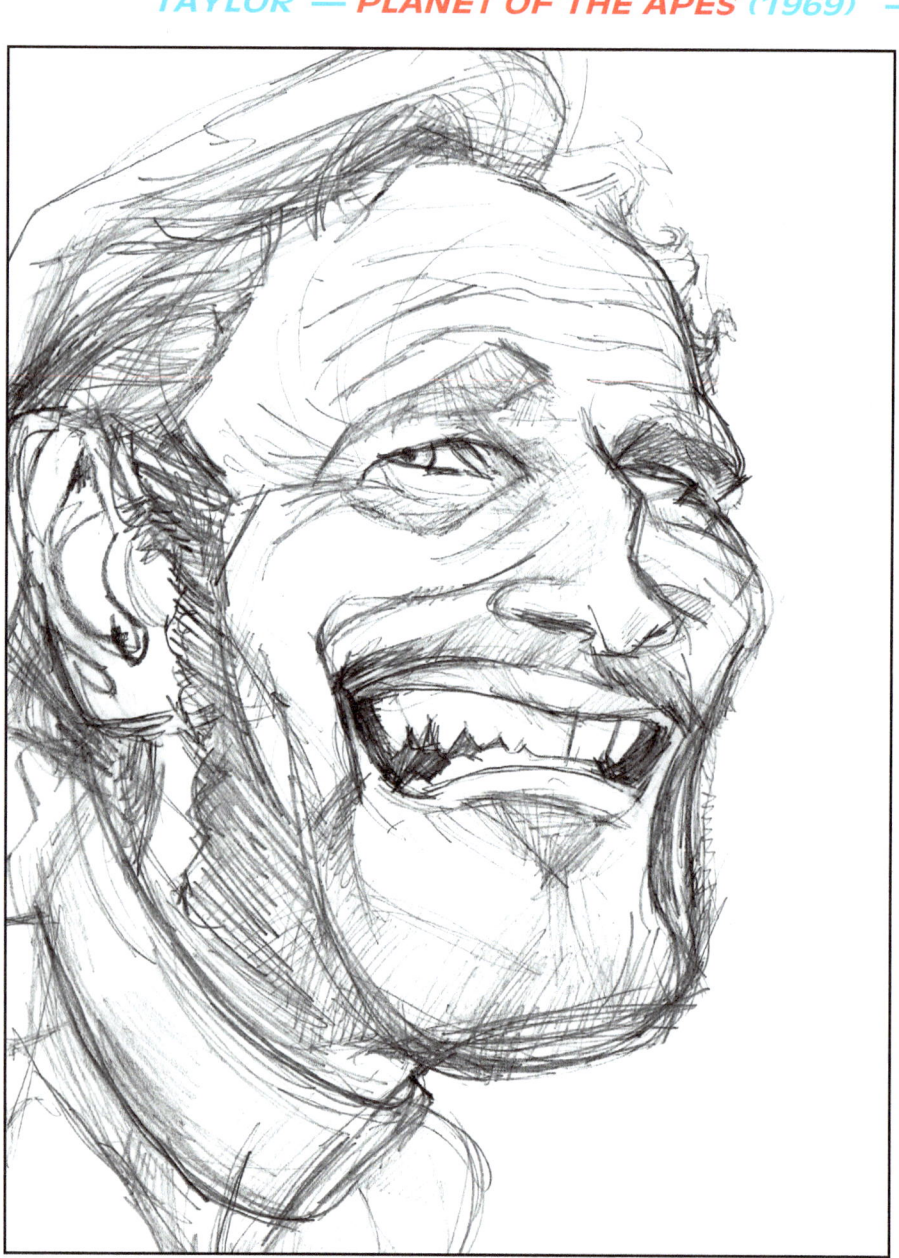

Poor Taylor. He crashlands on some crazy planet run by talking apes, his crew gets killed (why the brotha gotta get stuffed? That ain't right) and he gets shot in the throat so he can't even show the apes he can talk. Then later, after finally straightening all that out, he finds that the crazy planet he landed on is a post-apocalyptic earth, in one of the great twist endings of all time. With all that craziness, I have a hard time imagining anyone else other than the intense Charlton Heston in this role.

I didn't see *Planet of The Apes* in the theater (too young) but I did go to see two other Heston movies as a kid, the sci-fi flick *Omega Man* and the big blockbuster *Earthquake*. (Spoiler Alert!) Chuck dies at the end of both of them, which affected me greatly. The following is a verbatim exchange between myself and my older sister Paula at the end of *Earthquake*:

Me: Why did he jump back in?? He couldn't have saved her.

Paula (shrugging): He was in love.

Me (shaking head): That was STUPID.

Wow. So cynical for a nine year old. And Charlton Heston also dies in the sequel to *POTA*, the not so good *Beneath The Planet Of the Apes*. Man, to me as a kid, It seemed like he died in every movie he made in the 70's.

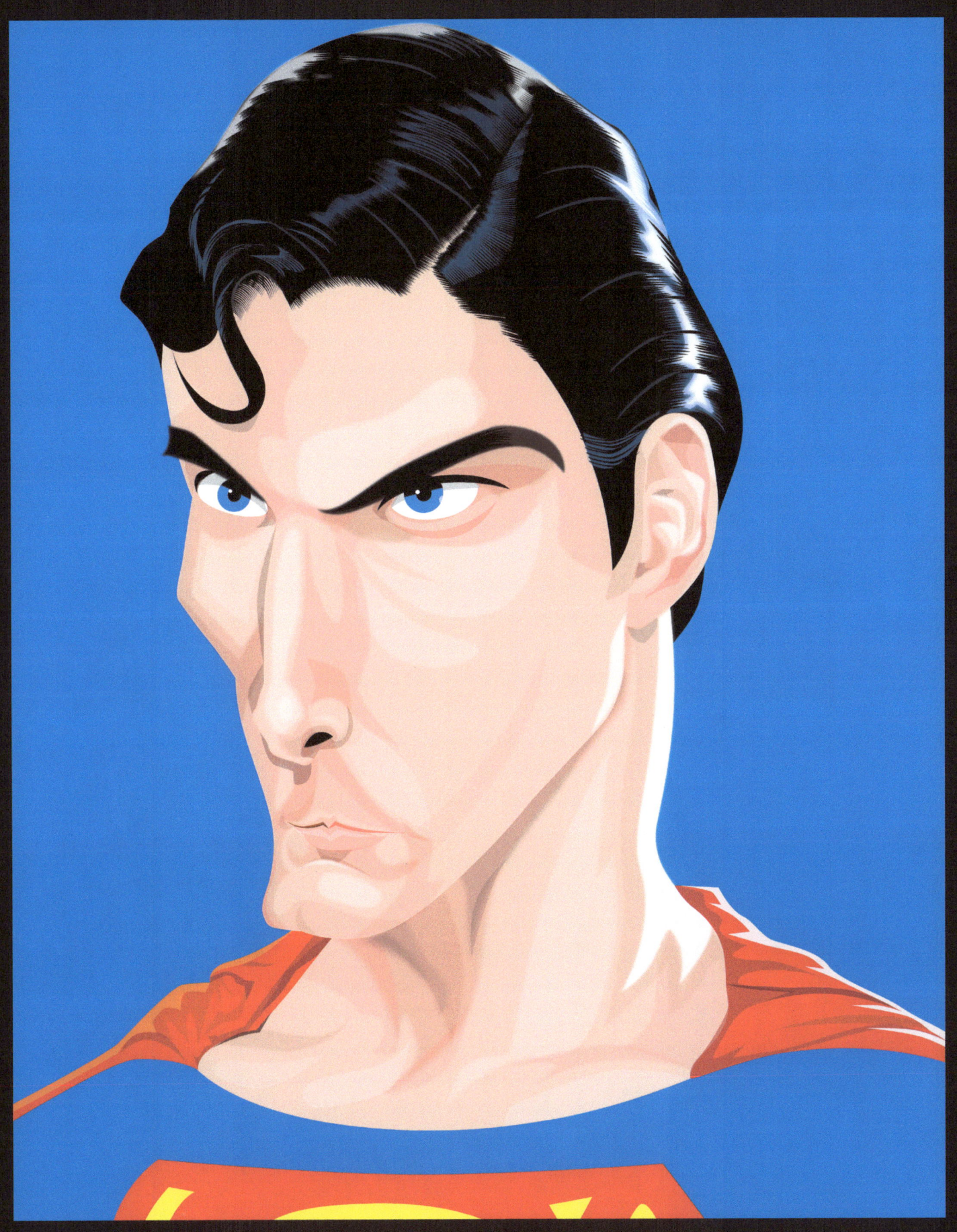

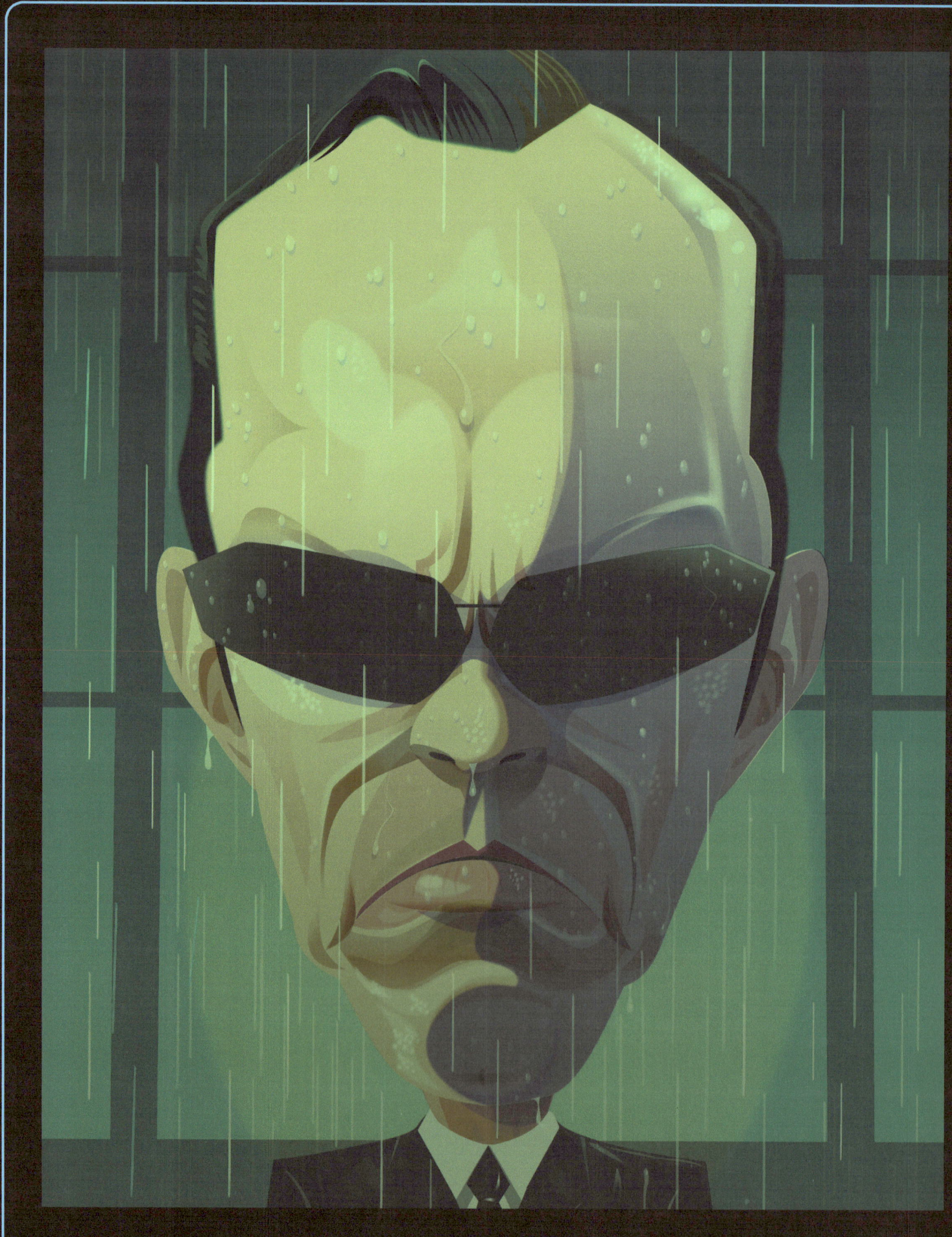

AGENT SMITH —— MATRIX REVOLUTIONS (2003)

"MIS-ter AND-erson." I love Hugo Weaving as Agent Smith. His disdain for not just the humans and the matrix but for, well, everything is really interesting to me. This image is from *Revolutions*, which I didn't see in the theater but something funny happened when I saw *The Matrix Reloaded.* I was sitting with my friend Tony Bourne and my wife Eda, who was five months pregnant at the time with my son William. This was at the Worldwide Cinema on 50th Street in Manhattan, which is a pretty nice theater. Anyway, the movie is going and there's a big fight scene and loud music and I look over at Eda and she is jammed up into the back of the seat like I was driving too fast or something. Apparently, all the noise was making William crazy and he was doing cartwheels and spinkicks in the womb, going all Neo and Eda just looked miserable. He was always really active before he was born, which was a tip off for the future. Poor Eda. I was talking to him through her stomach, trying to calm him down (I spoke to him a lot that way) but my man was amped by that movie. I'm almost afraid to show it to him now...

I really grew to like Princess Leia a lot in *The Empire Strikes Back.* In *Star Wars* I thought she was spunky but mildly annoying. Plus that hair is too much. In this she is still spunky but more likeable to me. I like how she is a real command presence in the rebellion and fighting her feelings for Han. Plus, that hair is a LOT better to look at.

I saw *TESB* at the Loews Astor Plaza in Manhattan, which was THE great place to see a movie back in the day. Huge theater and a huge crowd. And *Empire* didn't disappoint. I think I saw *Return of the Jedi* there as well. That, unfortunately, did disappoint.

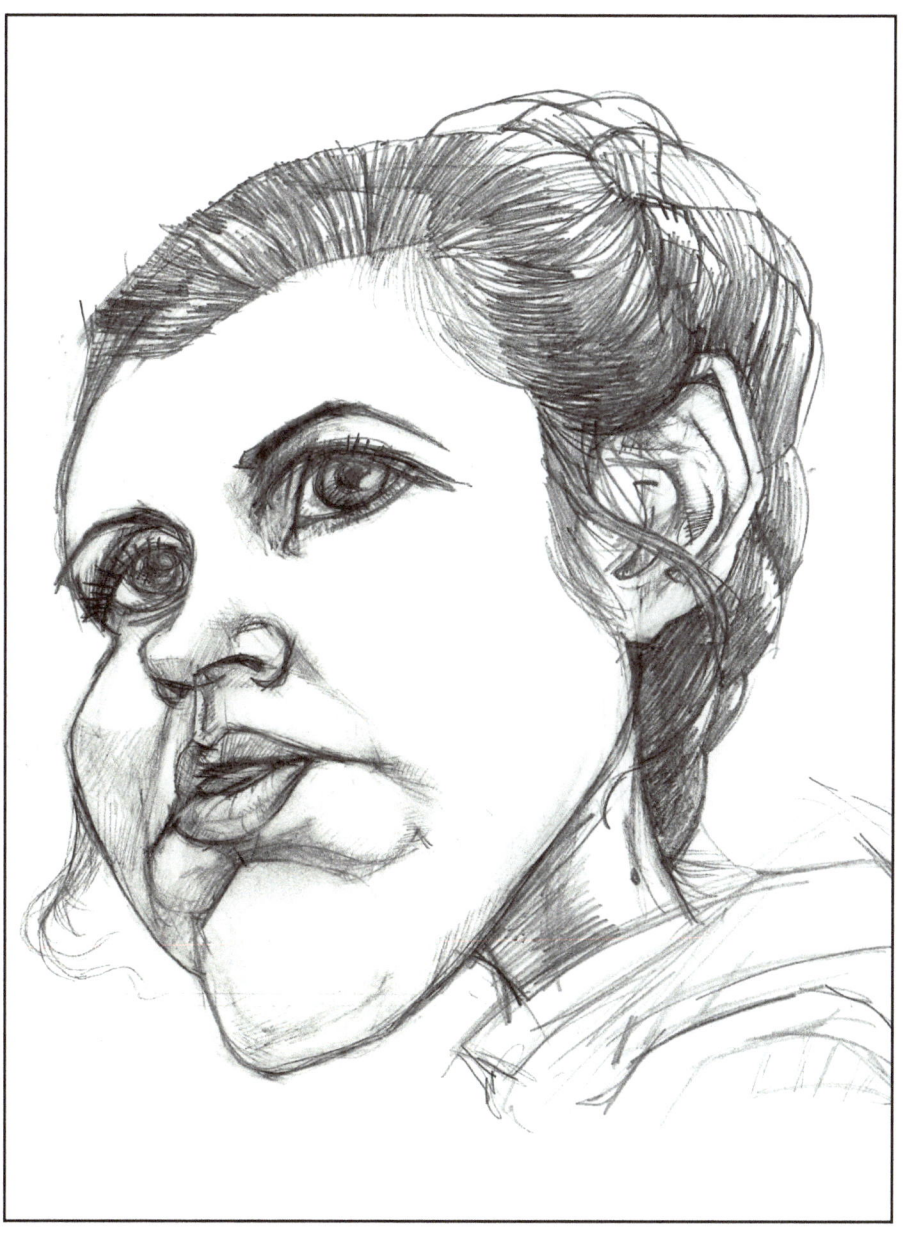

James Cameron is a genius. A lot of people probably won't want to admit that but he is. Instead of making a sequel exactly like the first movie he flips the script. He takes the "haunted house in space" concept of *Alien* and makes a bughunt thriller action movie with *Aliens*. And, realizing the star power of Arnold, he takes the villain from *Terminator* and makes him the hero in *T2*, squaring off against an even more powerful bad guy. It makes you wonder what he has in mind for his future Avatar films.

I love both of these movies. Not only does Arnold get to change but Linda Hamilton toughens up Sarah Conner, making her a Cameron warrior woman. But it's Schwarzenegger we're in the theater for and he's money in both movies. Plus there are plenty of Arnold lines from both flicks.to quote, although I tend to use the more obscure "Fug you, icehole!" from the first movie. Cursing with a German accent? Always fun.

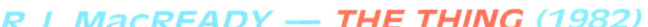

R.J. MacREADY — THE THING (1982)

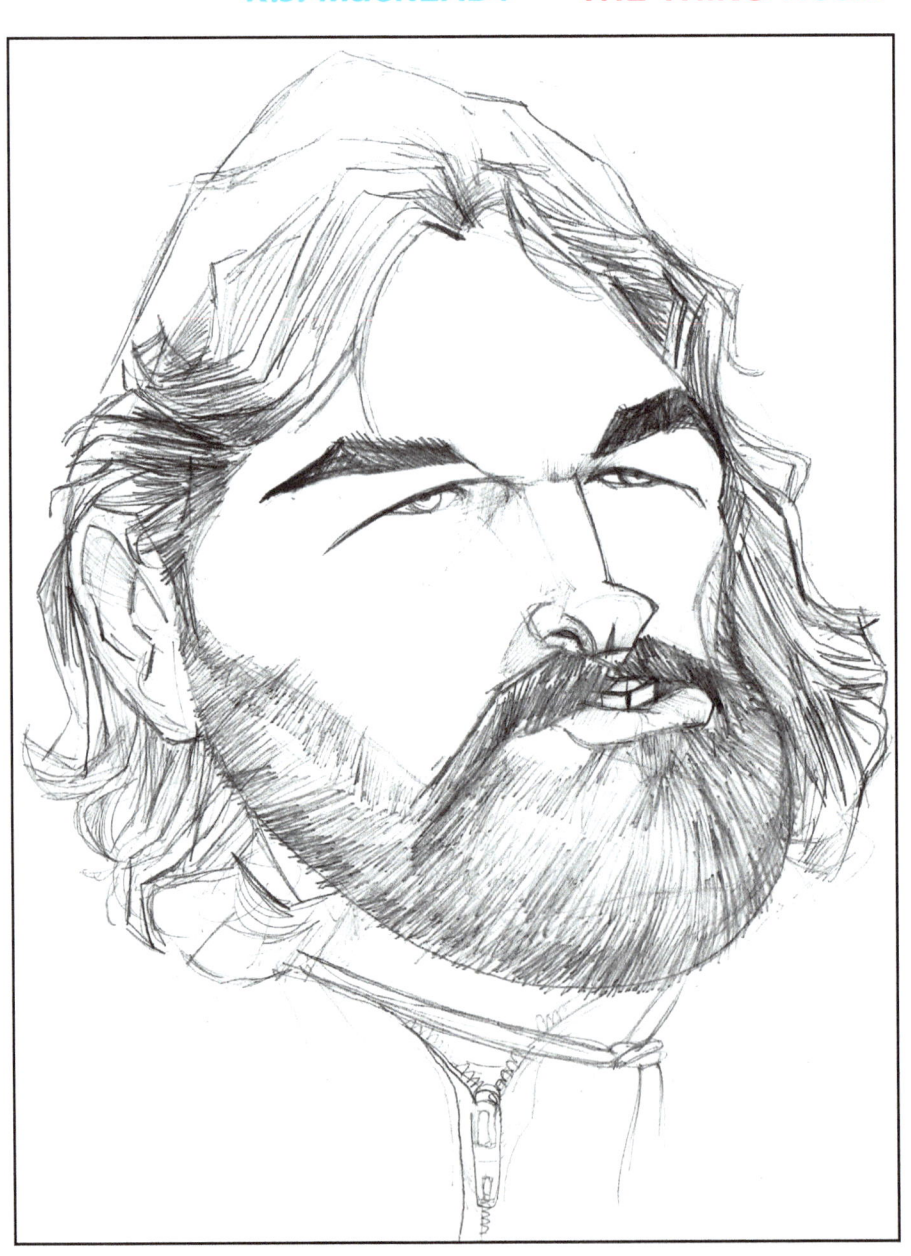

"I just cannot believe any of this voodoo bulls#&t!"

Yeah, it's crazy, Childs, but luckily you have the reliable and resourceful Mac on your side, despite his apparent inability to tell the difference between Norwegians and Swedes. I love *The Thing*. My main man André LeRoy Davis and I saw this in a double feature with *An American Werewolf In London* (That's a great double feature!) at The College, another long departed theater in Brooklyn. And Davis, a notorious night owl, stayed awake through both movies, so you know it was good (we saw *Blue Thunder* and André was out five minutes after the lights went down). Actually I love this version and the 1951 version, though they are very different. And just having Kurt Russell in anything instantly makes it better, even if it isn't that good (I'm one of the few people that thinks *Escape from New York* is dumb. But he's good in it.). This, though, is great already. And MacReady is a great sci-fi character.

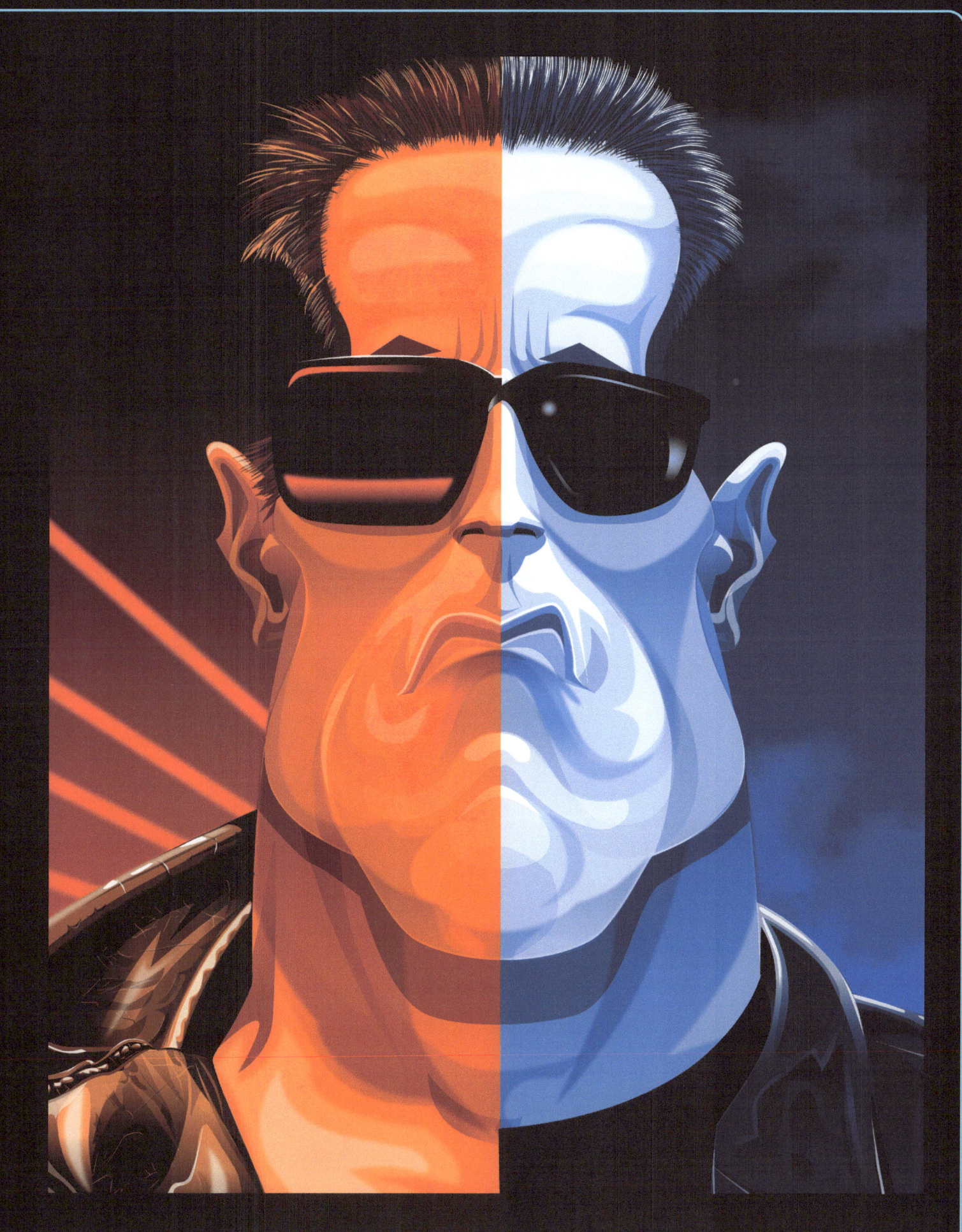

T-800 —— *THE TERMINATOR (1984)/T2(1992)* ——

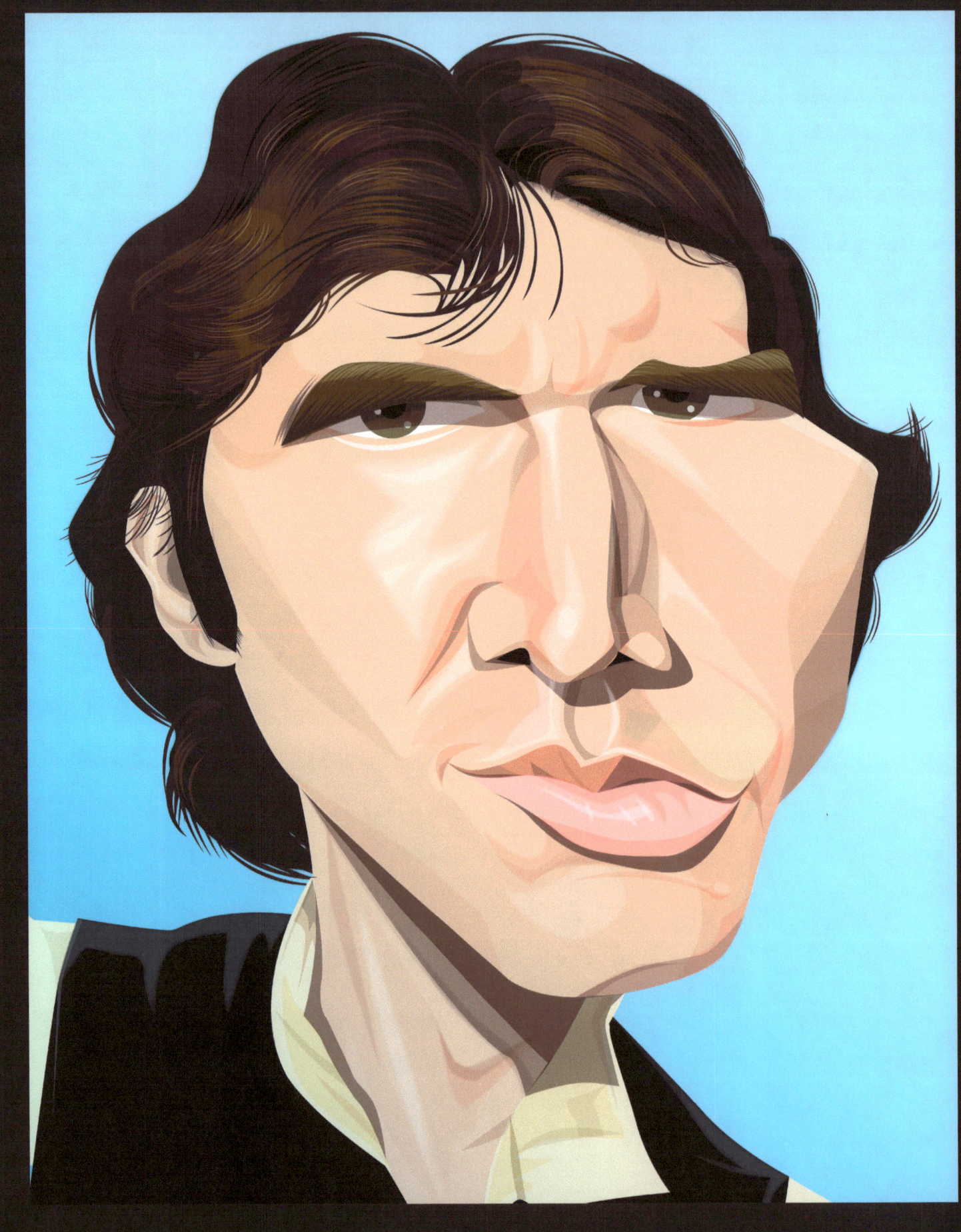

HAN SOLO ——— STAR WARS (1977)

I recently sat down and watched *Star Wars* and *The Empire Strikes Back* with my son (I refuse to call them Episodes 4 and 5). It was really cool seeing my son enjoying them so much. I hadn't seen either in awhile and I was reminded of how good they are and, in particular, how enjoyable Harrison Ford is as Han Solo. He's funny, biting, annoying, heroic, selfish... what a great character. He has a lot of good lines but one of my favorites is a very simple one from *Empire*, right before he kisses Leia for the first time. She's complaining about how difficult he makes things and he very sarcastically and condescendingly says "I do, I really do." Lol.. Such a smart ass. Han is cool. And he DID shoot first, dammit.

THE OPERATIVE — SERENITY (2005)

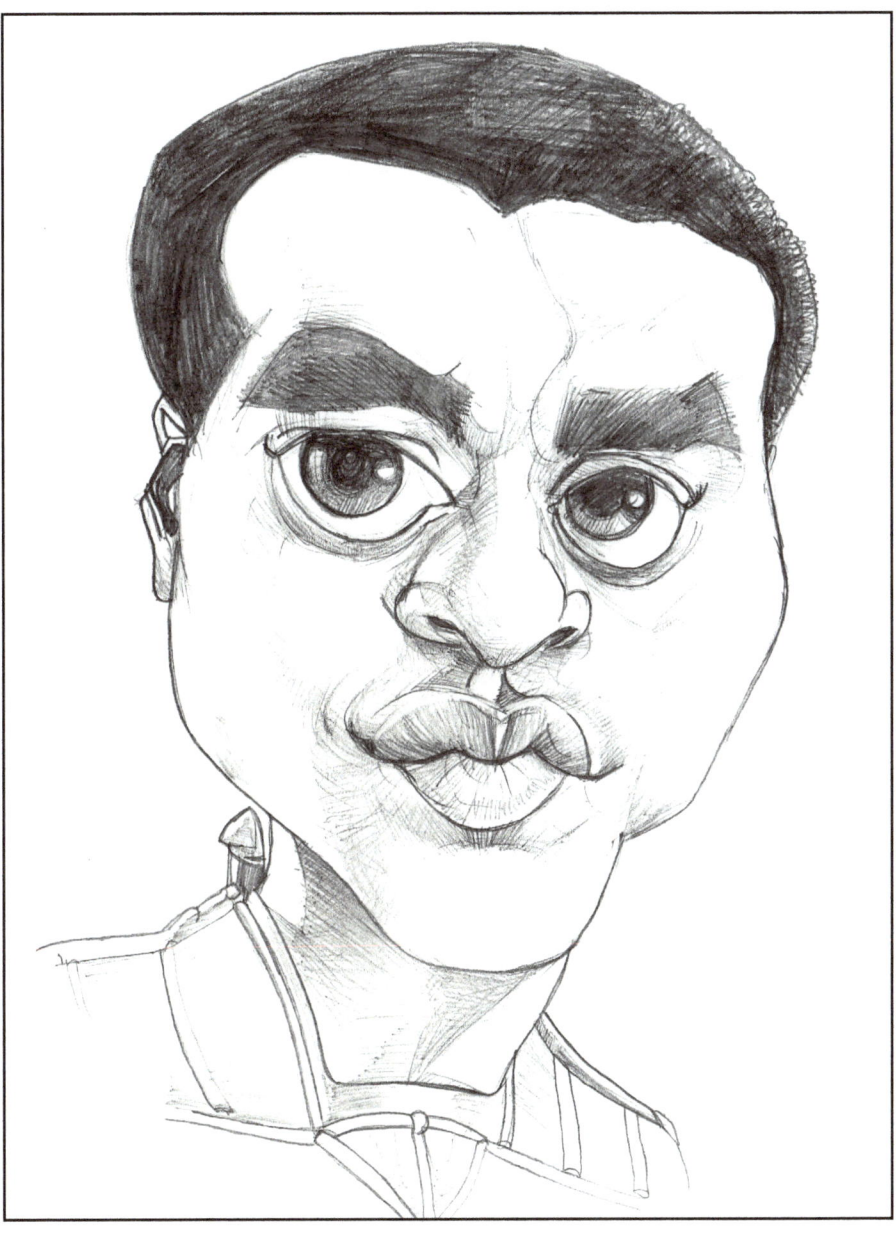

The Operative, as portrayed by the great Chiwetel Ejiofor, is the rarest of movie villains: one that actually knows his place in the universe. When asked by Mal if the *Serenity* crew has to die so that the Operative can live in his better world he replies "I'm not going to live there. There's no place for me there... any more than there is for you. Malcolm...I'm a monster. What I do is evil. I have no illusions about it, but it must be done." Him knowing this, of course, makes him that much more dangerous as he wrecks Mal's world to protect a dark secret that the Alliance has. But even a blunt instrument knows when the battle is lost and he ultimately helps Mal and company (what's left of them) to survive. And off the Operative goes to face an uncertain future. What do you do when you don't know your place anymore?

I thought Chris Pine made a very good James T. Kirk in the new *Star Trek*. Played as more rebellious and careless because he didn't have his father in this timeline, Pine got to push the character in different directions but you could still see the essence of Kirk coming through. I enjoyed the movie, although it came across like a Cliff Notes version of a *Trek* movie sometimes, which may not necessarily be a bad thing.The nexy movie is right on the top of my list as most anticipated sci-fi flicks coming out. It'll be good to see Pine in the gold shirt for the whole movie this time.

COMMANDER J. J. ADAMS — *FORBIDDEN PLANET* (1956)

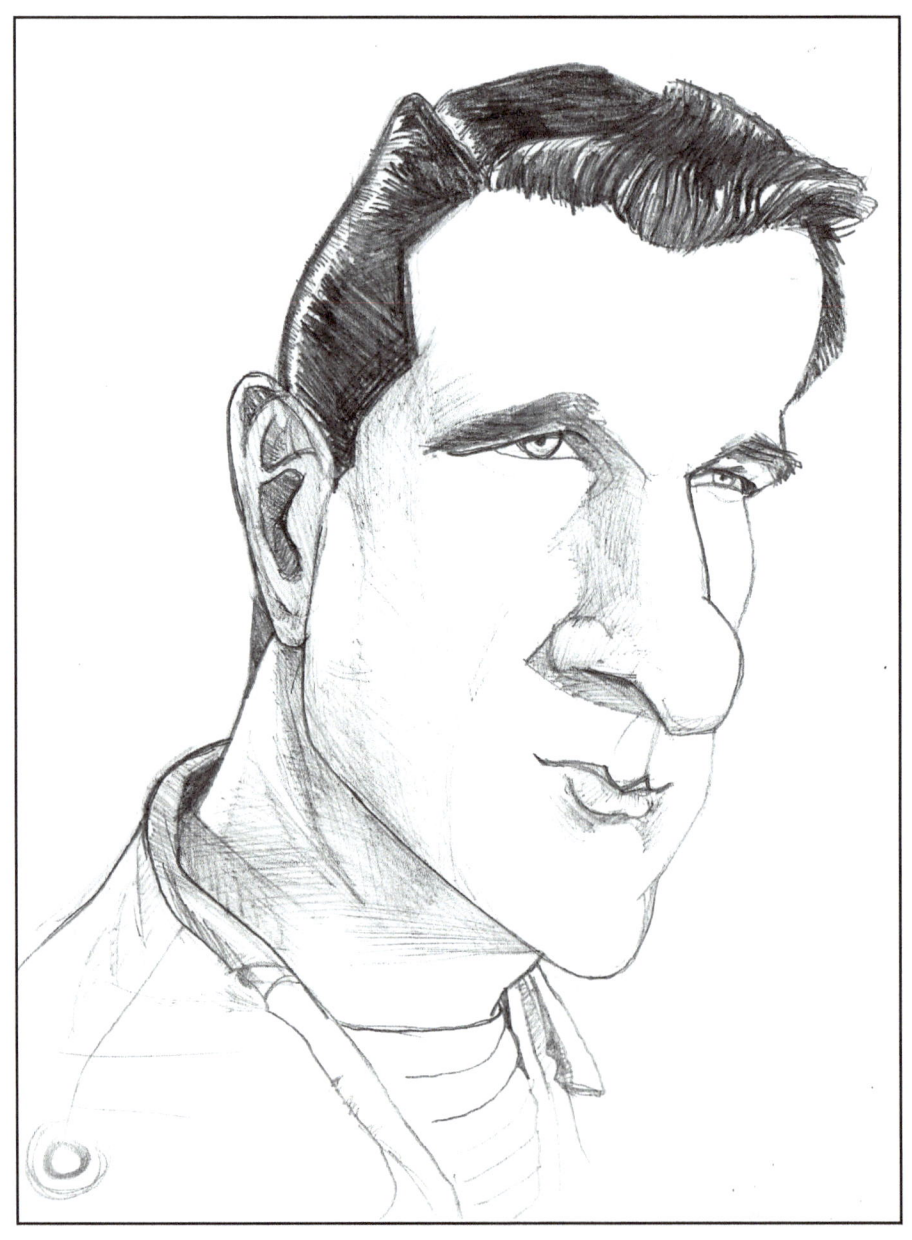

I love '50's science fiction movies. Even if they are bad they are worth watching. But there are so many good ones that I grew up on. *Kronos. The Beast From 20,000 Fathoms. It Came From Outer Space. When Worlds Collide. This Island Earth. War of the Worlds. The Day The Earth Stood Still.* The list goes on and on. But my three favorites from that decade are *The Thing From Another World, Them!* and this film, *Forbidden Planet.* You can see where *Star Trek* came from when you watch this movie. Leslie Nielsen (yup, that same Leslie Nielsen a.k.a. Frank Drebin) is a very good commander, definitely Pike and Kirk before there ever was. And his relationship with the doctor and his executive officer is definitely *Trek* like. I love this movie. They spent money and made an intelligent, great film. *Forbidden Planet* is definitely on my Hook Movie List. If I turn on the TV and it's on, I'm hooked.

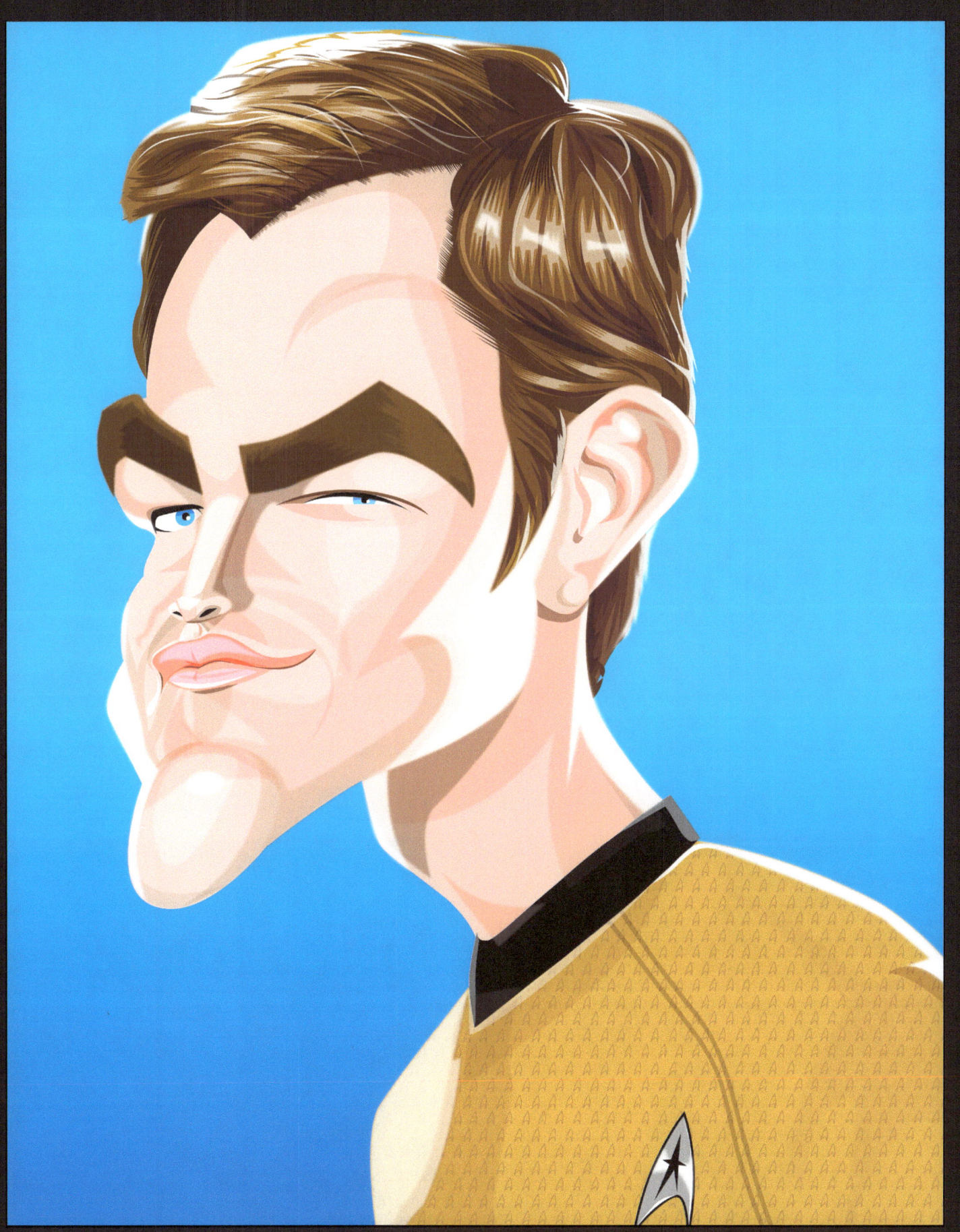

CAPTAIN JAMES T. KIRK ── *STAR TREK* (2009) ──

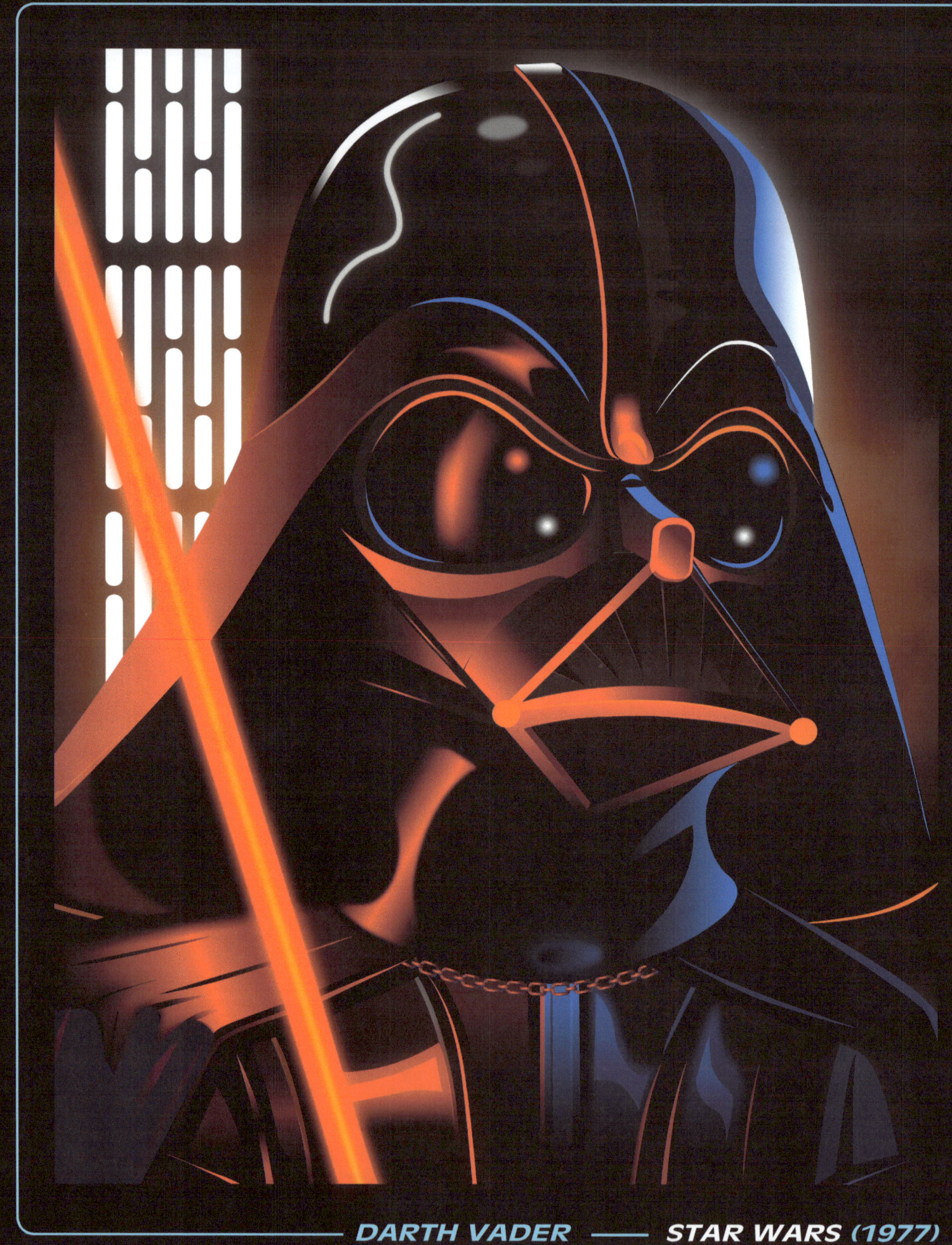

DARTH VADER —— STAR WARS (1977)

Obviously, Darth Vader is one of the great villains of all time. The black helmet, the cape, the breathing.... but it's the voice of James Earl Jones that puts it all over the top. Recently I was at my son's school to drop him off early in the morning and I hung out for while as I often do. The before school care program is run by the beloved Mr. Joe and this morning in particular he put on a DVD called *Disney American Legends* hosted by James Earl Jones. The kids didn't seem very interested until Jones appeared on screen and started speaking. This one little boy heard him and said "Hey! It's Darth Vader!" and all of a sudden there were ten kids watching this movie. Sometimes, the voice makes all the difference.

ALEX MURPHY/ROBOCOP — *ROBOCOP (1987)*

I saw *Robocop* at the Metropolitan on Fulton Street in Brooklyn which was, besides the Sunrise out on Long Island, the rowdiest movie theater I've ever been in. If you didn't like people talking back to the screen or missing entire scenes of dialogue because of the noise, then the Metropolitan was not the theater for you. Actually, silly me, I DO like hearing entire scenes of dialogue. The Met is one of the reasons I started going to the movies almost exclusively in Manhattan. But I'm glad I saw *Robocop* there. That was a spirited crowd that got dead silent when Peter Weller's character is brutally executed (or so the bad guys thought). To this day I still laugh at this; if you remember, the movie goes dark after Weller gets shot in the head and then there are short bursts of static before we realize that we are seeing through Robocop's eyes.. But just before we found that out that some angry guy turned to the projection booth and shouted "Hey man, fix the f*$&in' movie!!!" Ah, the good ol' Metropolitan.

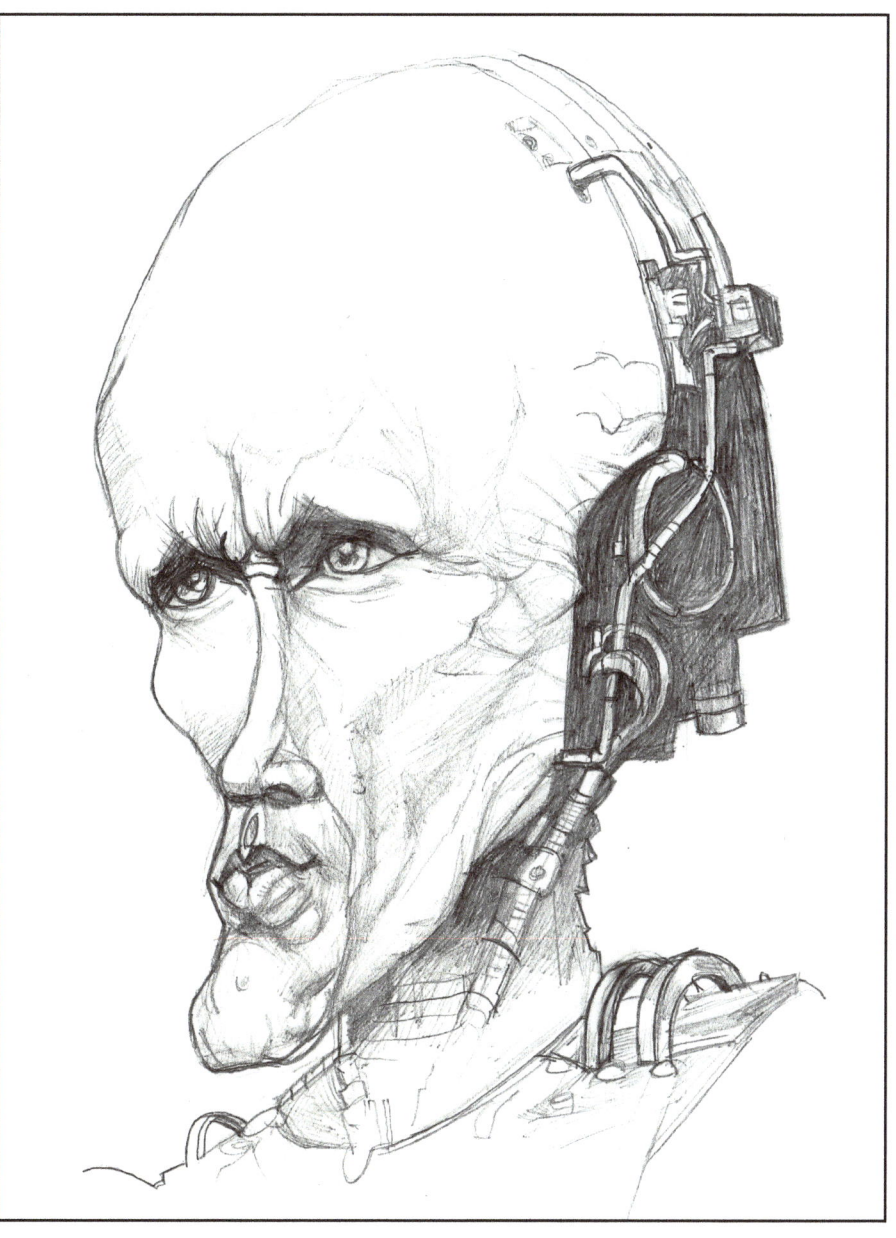

I don't remember where I saw *The Matrix* or who I saw it with, if anyone. It may have been my friend Tony Bourne. It may have been on Route 440 in New Jersey. Not sure. There are a few movies like that where I have no recollection of where I saw them. *Star Trek II. Ghostbusters, Superman II.* Can't remember. Well, it can't be because of the quality of the movie. I really enjoyed those films and *The Matrix* as well, which bugged me the hell out when I saw it. I had no idea what the movie was about before I saw it (hardly anyone did. They kept a serious lid on the plot) so I was just blown away by it. And Laurence Fishburne was perfect as Morpheus, all wise and knowing and wearing cool sh*!. I wasn't crazy about the sequels, though. I think The Wachowski's lost the handle on them, unfortunately, but the first movie is definitely one of science fiction's most influential films.

CAPTAIN CHRISTOPHER PIKE — STAR TREK (1965)

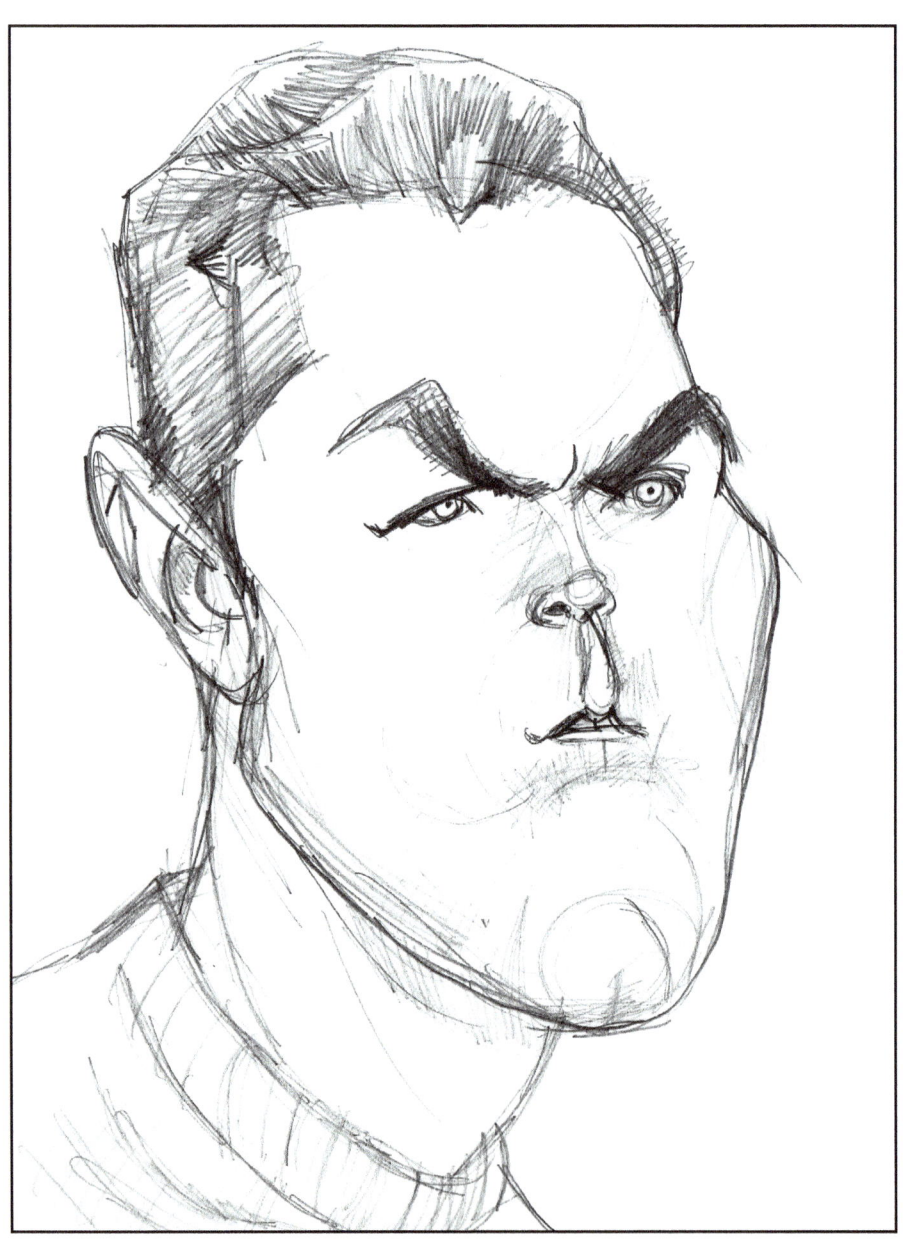

If you were going to make a guy that visually represented the perfect Starfleet captain, you would make Jeffrey Hunter. The guy just looks the part. And he was very good. Of course, NBC said that the original *Star Trek* pilot "The Cage" was "too cerebral" and asked for another one. Jeffrey Hunter bailed and William Shatner took over. But, no offense to Shatner, it would've been cool to see Hunter as Pike while the show was retooled. *Star Trek* would be completely different today if he had stuck around. Unfortunately, Hunter, due to a head injury, would be dead 4 years later. Luckily, they reused the entire pilot footage and we can still enjoy his performance as Captain Christopher Pike. Jeffrey Hunter will always be a part of *Star Trek*.

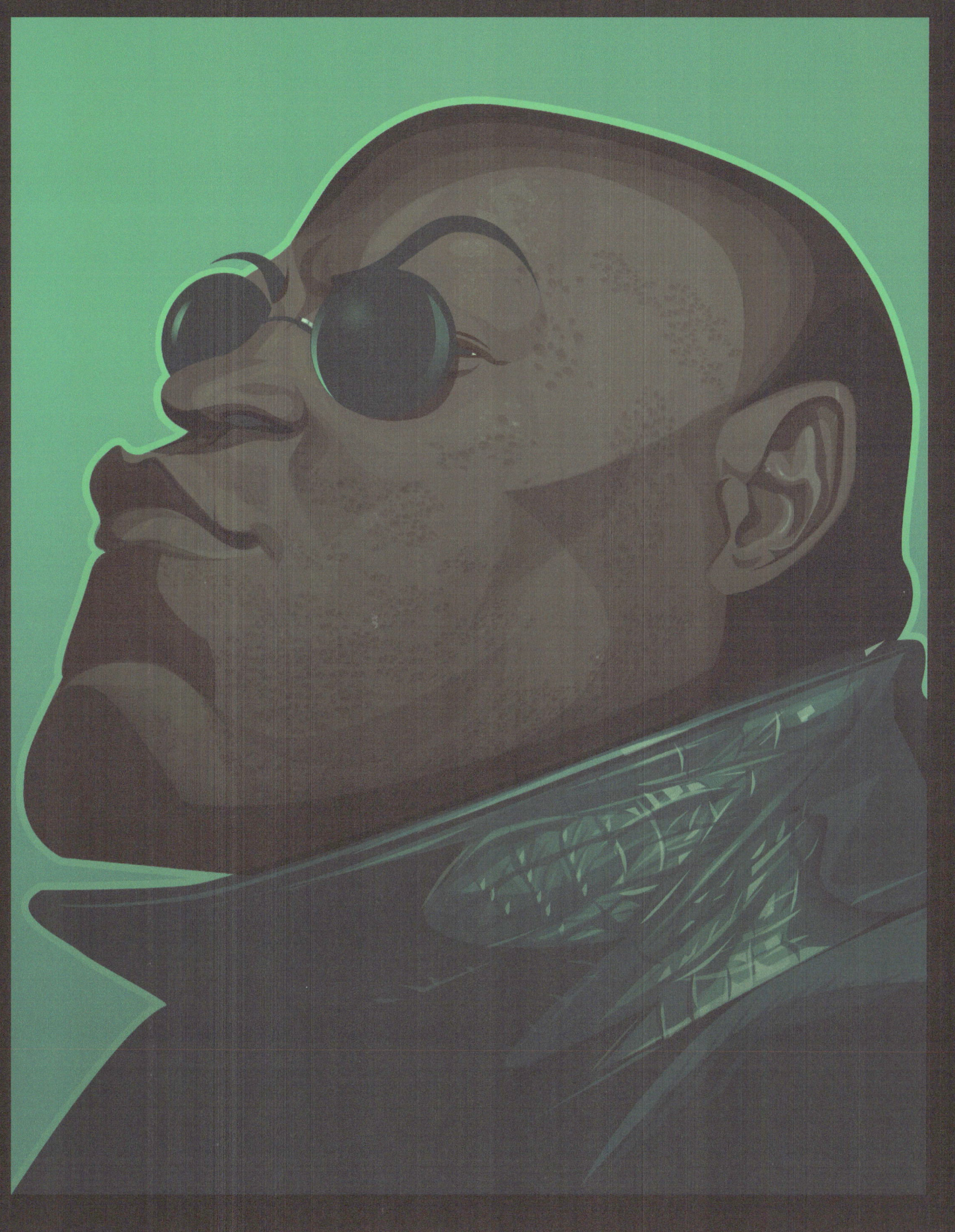

MORPHEUS ——— *THE MATRIX (1999)* ———

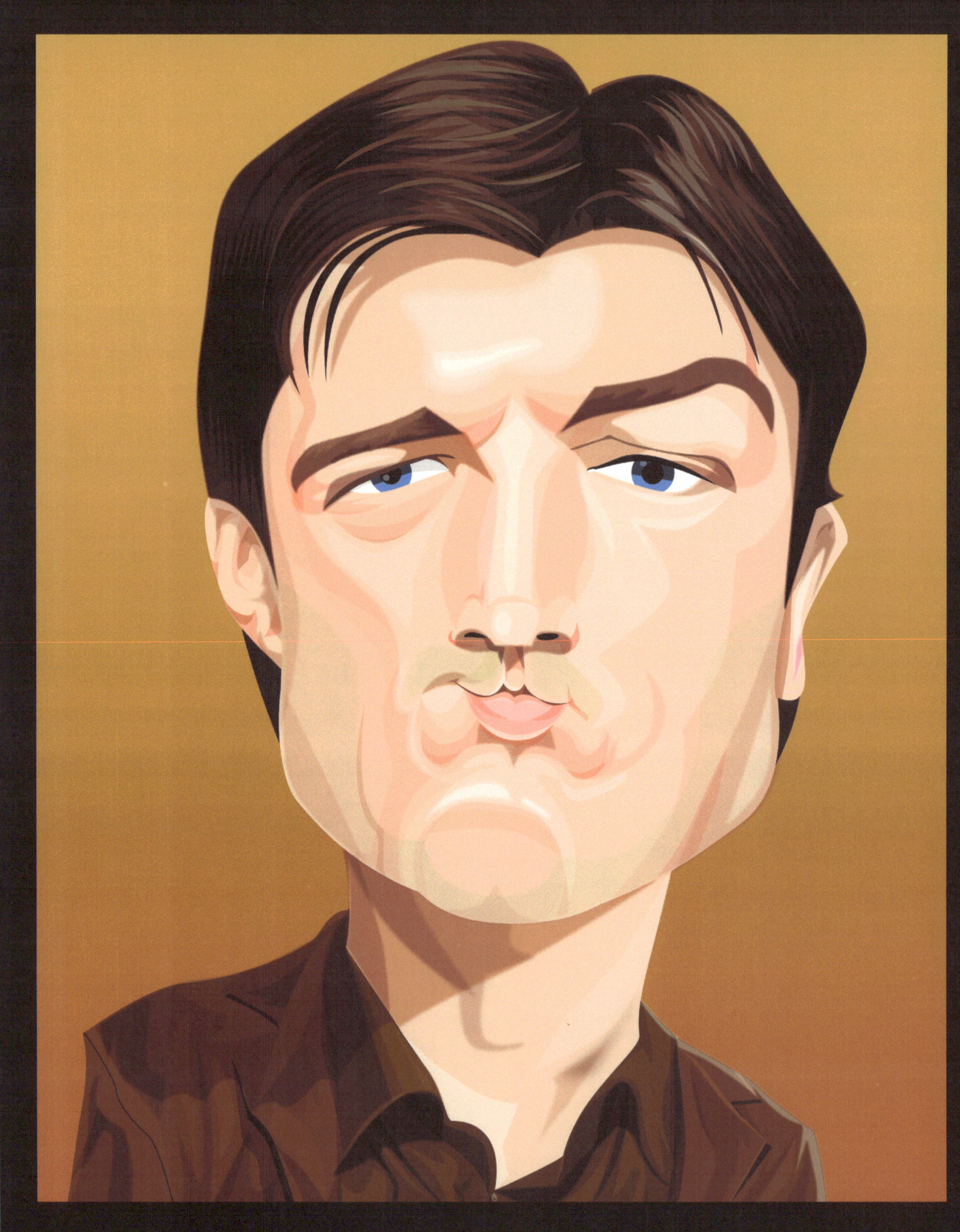

CAPTAIN MALCOLM REYNOLDS ── FIREFLY (2002)

Ah, *Firefly*... Despite only having 14 episodes this show stayed with everyone who watched it.. and that's what got the movie *Serenity* made. Great characters (led by Nathan Fillion as the contradictory and complicated war hero turned outlaw Mal Reynolds) and great stories made this show so easy to love. Boy, I really, really wish it were still on. *Firefly* and *Farscape* (which at one point used to air back to back on Friday nights - that was a great two hours right there) are the only two shows I ever wrote letters complaining about their cancellation. Didn't do a whole lot of good... but then again, we did get the *Serenity* and *Farscape: the Peacekeeper Wars* movies. That's better than not seeing these fun characters like Mal ever again.

QUI-GON JINN — THE PHANTOM MENACE (1999)

I must admit, I am not a big fan of *The Phantom Menace* (I'm not really a big fan of any *Star Wars* movie made after *The Empire Strikes Back*). To be honest, I've never seen the movie from beginning to end. It just doesn't hold my attention. And that Jar Jar Binks is unwatchable. But I do like Liam Neeson as Qui-Gon Jinn. I mean it's Liam Neeson. He brings validity to any movie. My friend Jon Goldmacher, who is the biggest Star Wars fan I know personally, actually doesn't like Liam Neeson. Who doesn't like Liam Neeson? Besides Jon, that is. Then again, Jon doesn't like mushrooms so... there you have it. Liam Neeson. Mushrooms. Synonymous.

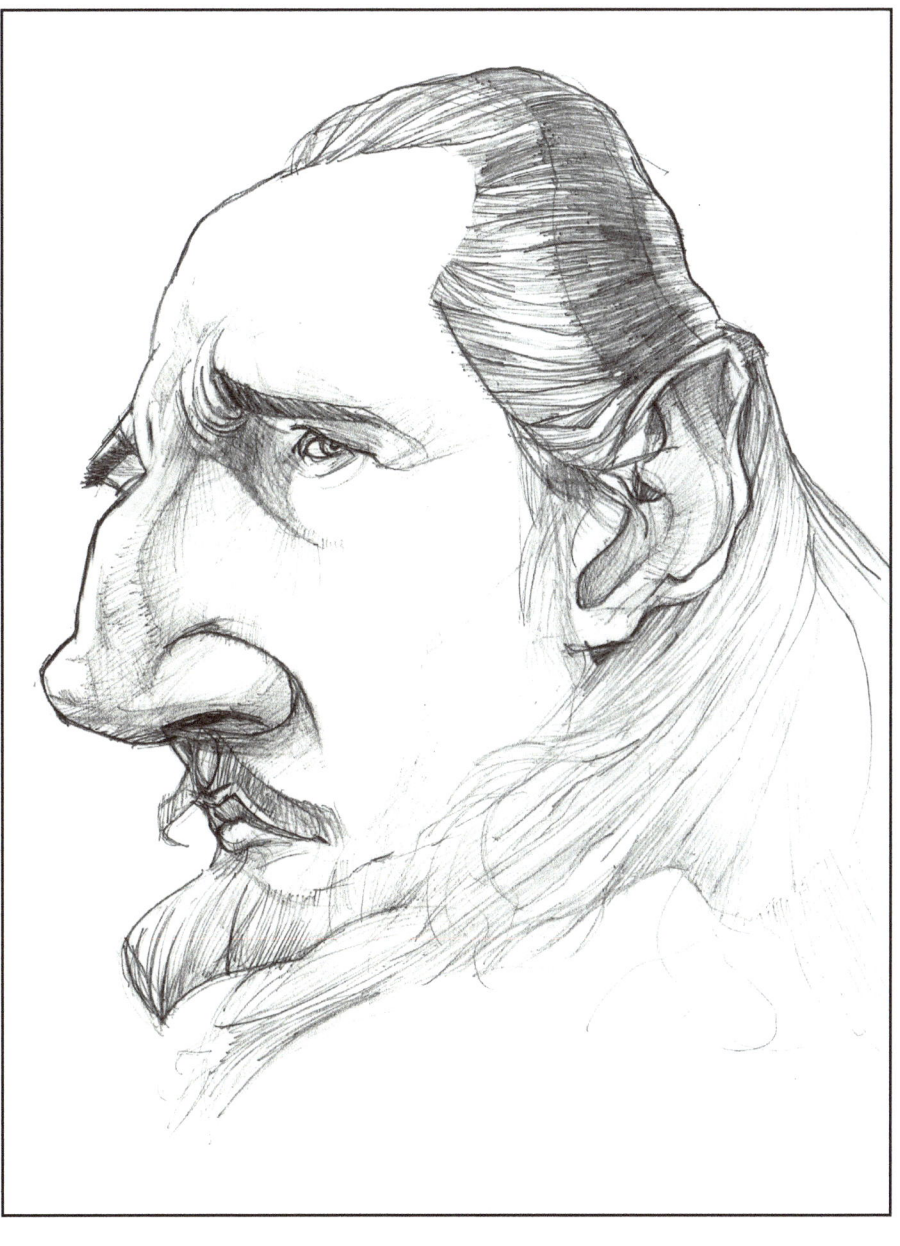

As a kid I used to watch *Doctor Who* on Channel 13 in New York with Tom Baker. I love British sci-fi. It is so much different than American sc-fi. Less formulaic. So when *Doctor Who* came back I was anxious to see it. And Christopher Eccleston was very good as the ninth Doctor, all leather jacketed and edgy. I was really disappointed when I found out he was leaving and I was VERY leery about this David Tennant guy. BOY, was I wrong. The Tenth Doctor is far and away my favorite. And I really like Matt Smith. But Tennant just owned it. His Doctor was a little more fun-loving and goofy than Eccleston's but he has a serious dark side (as seen in the episodes "Runaway Bride" and "The Family of Blood"). Tennant rules. And "Blink"? That was one of the best episodes of any sci-fi show I've ever seen.

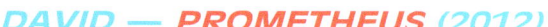

DAVID — PROMETHEUS (2012)

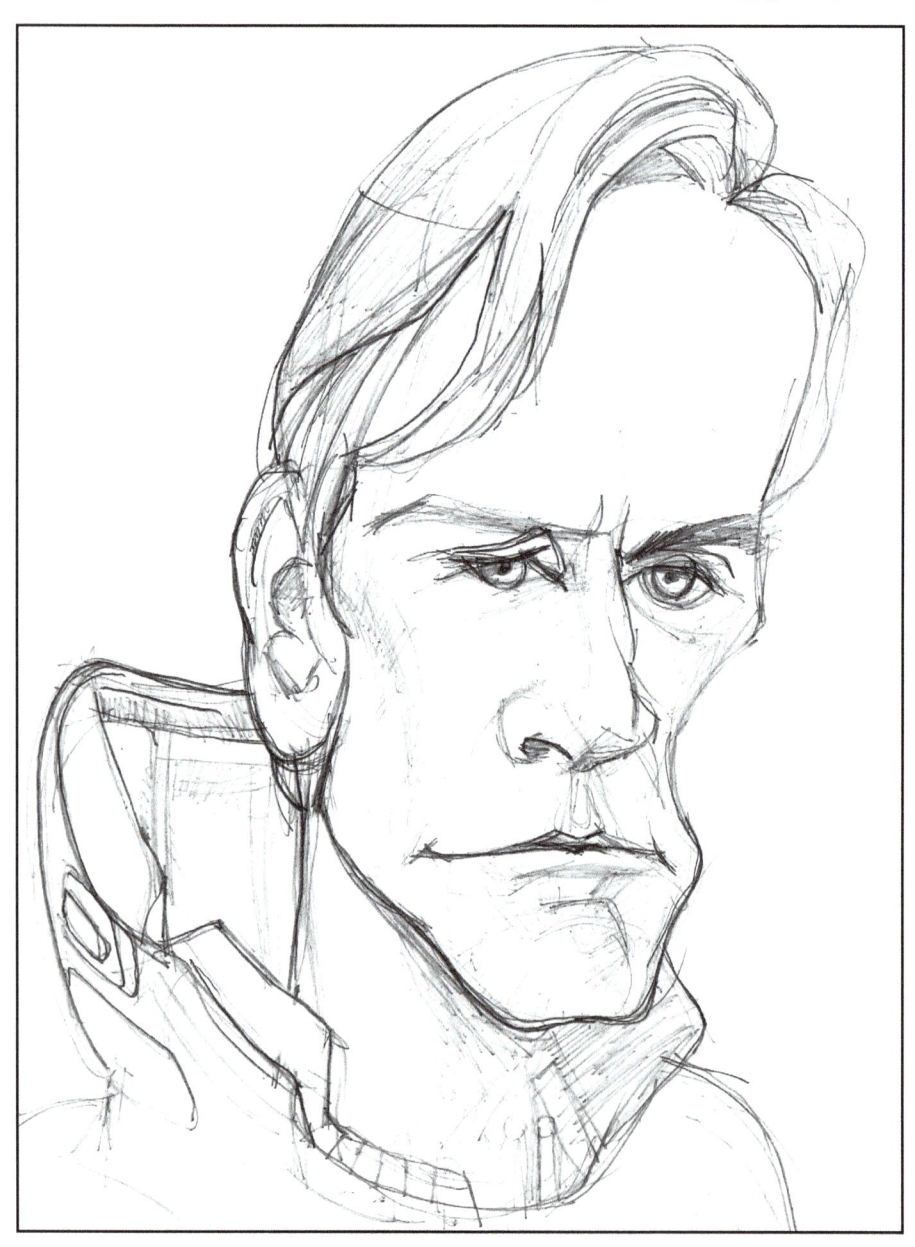

Yeah, I was disappointed in *Prometheus.* I didn't hate it but I wanted to love it and I just couldn't. Too many characters that I didn't care about ended up doing too many stupid things for me to truly get behind the movie. Sometimes the film, with all that was happening and people's apparent obliviousness, seemed to be taking place on three different ships. And then came a part where it seems like Ridley Scott and the screenwriters said "Oh yeah, we gotta kill half the crew before the end." However, I did like Shaw and Vickers as characters, especially Shaw (that medical pod scene with her is just insane). But David, as played by Michael Fassbender, really made the movie for me. He is very conflicted, his motivations very muddled. His clear contempt for human beings is at odds with his programmed need to serve Peter Weyland regardless of the cost. He's like a walking Hal 9000. But he was fascinating to watch. Does he warn Shaw of approaching danger because he is intrigued by her or, selfishly, so she can save him in return? Don't know. But Fassbender is so good you almost don't care.

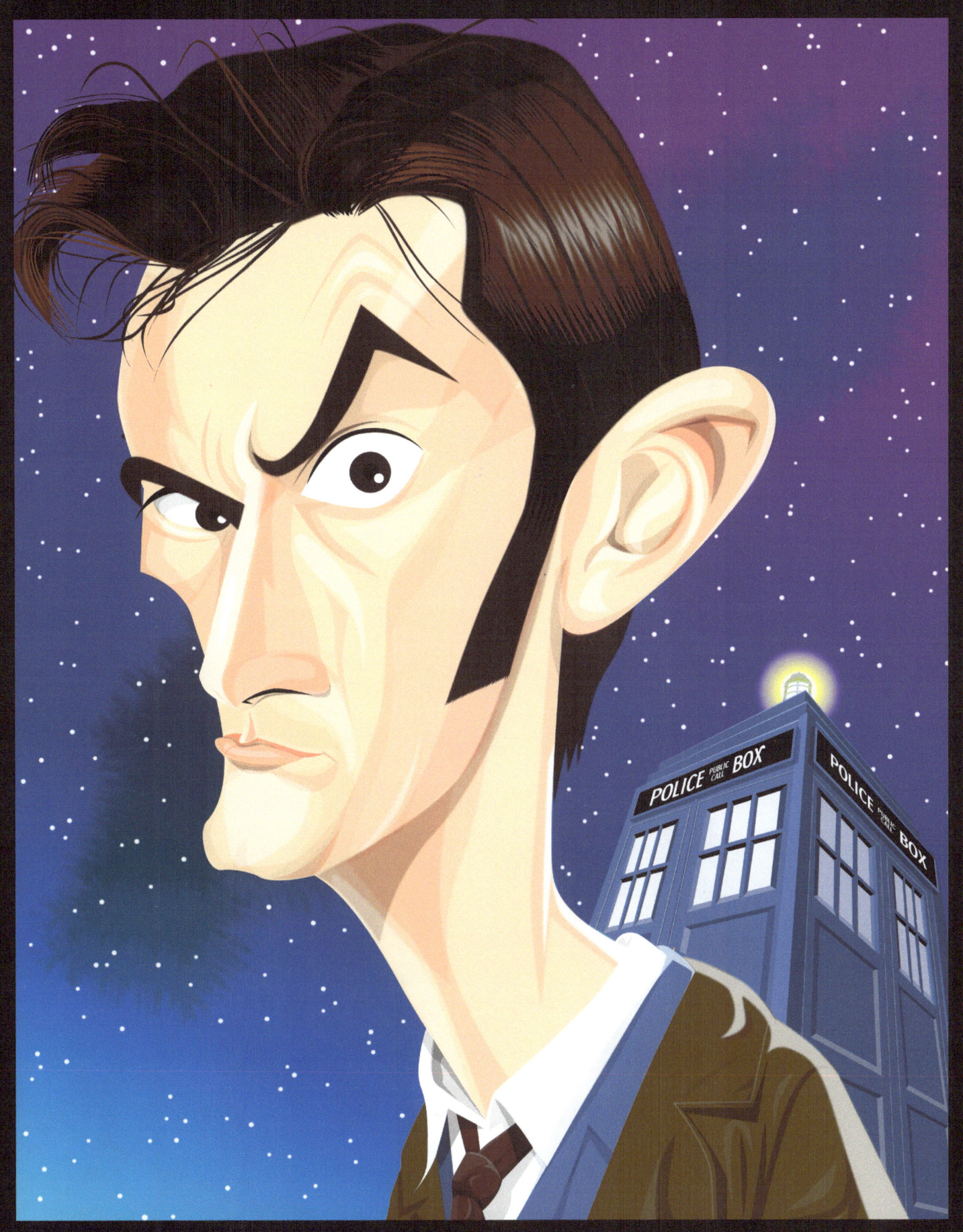

THE TENTH DOCTOR —— DOCTOR WHO (2005-2010)

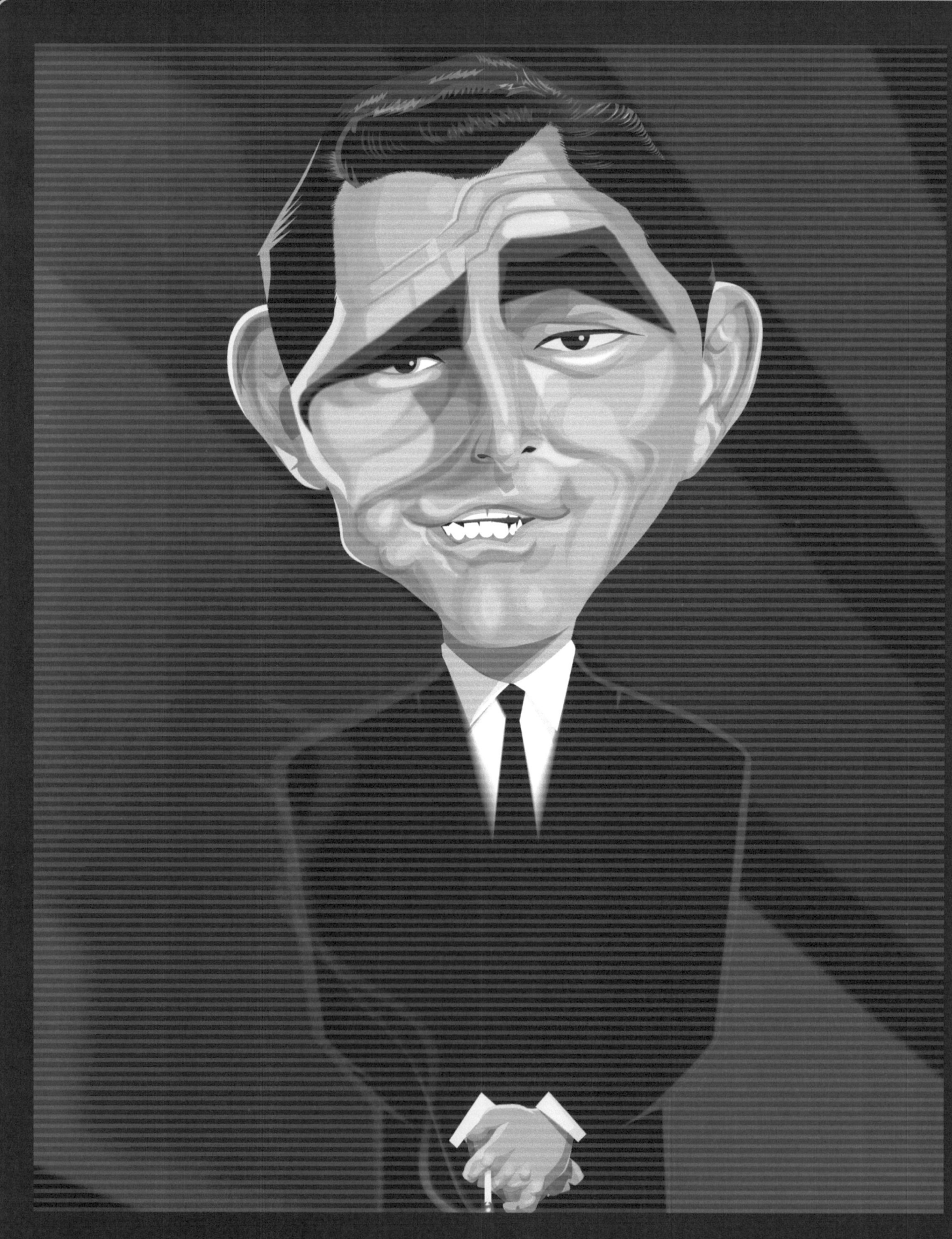

ROD SERLING ——— **THE TWILIGHT ZONE (1959-1964)**

"There is a fifth dimension beyond that which is known to man. It is a dimension as vast as space and as timeless as infinity. It is the middle ground between light and shadow, between science and superstition, and it lies between the pit of man's fears and the summit of his knowledge. This is the dimension of imagination. It is an area which we call the Twilight Zone."

That is the first season (and my favorite) opening narration by Rod Serling and there was nothing better than sitting in a dark room watching Channel 11 late at night and hearing this. I know, I know, Rod Serling is not a fictional character (although he does play a small funny part at the end of the episode "A World Of His Own") but I have to acknowledge his effect on me. *The Twilight Zone* is one of my favorite television shows and Serling, Richard Matheson, Charles Beaumont and other writers crafted a different, crazy world every episode in a variety of genres for me to get lost in. There were sci-fi episodes like "Third From The Sun", "The Invaders", "And When The Sky Was Opened" and "Elegy" where maybe now the science is wacky but the fiction is still great. Thank you, Mr. Serling, for scaring the crap out of a thrilled young kid way, way after dark.

Well, that's it. Because of time constraints SO many characters I wanted to draw did not make this book. Aeryn Sun. Commander Koenig and Doctor Helena Carter. TOS Spock. Loki. Black Widow, Mulder and Scully. Miss Namikawa from *Monster Zero* (really wanted that one in, needed to give a Godzilla movie some love). Oh well. Are you interested in seeing another book? And maybe seeing those characters I mentoned or some other ones? Visit me at kgreene.deviantart.com or on Facebook at www.facebook.com/heroesandvillainsbook and let me know if another book is a good idea and who you would like to see! And thank you for your support!